PRAYING AN

PRAYING AND SINGING

J.D. Crichton

COLLINS

Collins Liturgical Publications
187 Piccadilly, London W1V 9DA

First published 1980.
© J.D. Crichton 1980. All rights reserved.
ISBN 0 00 599646 5

Nihil obstat Anton Cowan *Censor*
Imprimatur David Norris VG
Westminster 12 November, 1979

Made and printed in Great Britain by
William Collins Sons and Co, Glasgow
Typeset in Baskerville, by Westholme Graphics Ltd, Cambs.

Offered to
The Lady Abbess and Community
of
Stanbrook Abbey
who have done so much for the liturgy
for so long

Contents

Preface

This small book had its origin in two talks I was invited to give to the Panel of Monastic Musicians meeting at Douai Abbey in January, 1979. It was agreed that the title of the talks should be 'Music and Liturgy: Problems and Opportunities'. I undertook the assignment with great diffidence. I am not a musician, but I know enough about the complexities of the subject to realise that I might very well be intruding where angels fear to tread. The distinguished audience did not tear me to pieces as I rather feared they would and I came away with the impression – which may be an illusion born of their kindly attention – that at least some of the things I had said were worth saying. I have therefore completely re-written the talks and offer the result, still with diffidence, to a wider public.

Two notions dominate the book. The first is that in planning and writing music for the liturgy musicians and composers should examine the literary forms of the texts to be used. This seems to be in accord not only with the nature of the liturgy but with the explicit requirements of the church. The second notion is that the function or role of the texts in the liturgical celebration should be understood and respected. Both views find support in an injunction of the General Instruction to the Roman Missal:

'The style of utterance of the priest's texts, those of his assistants and of the congregation should be suited to the *nature of the text concerned,* according as it is a reading, a prayer, a directive, an acclamation or a hymn; it should take into account also the form of the celebration and its degree of solemnity. *The characteristics of the different languages and sensibilities of the different peoples also have a bearing on this matter'* (no. 18).

If this is applicable to those texts that are usually spoken, *a fortiori* it is applicable to sung texts.

The fundamental reason for this is that music in the liturgy has a *munus ministeriale* to perform; it is at the service of the community, and of this too I have spoken. It may seem to be a limiting factor, and of course it is, but great art has been created in the past when it has been limited by tradition, by convention or by the requirements of the client.

The translations of the two documents used in this book, namely the Constitution on the Liturgy (CL) and the General Instruction to the Roman Missal (GIRM), are those of Father Clifford Howell, S.J. The second is published by the C.T.S., 1973.

Finally, I would like to thank the Panel of Monastic Musicians for giving me the stimulus to think about this matter and for their indulgent reception of what I had to say.

The Feast of St Wulstan, January 1979   J.D.C.

CHAPTER I

Music and Liturgy: Problems and Opportunities

It is now something like thirteen years since we began living in an age of liturgical change. The first change came in 1965 when permission was given for most of the Mass to be celebrated in English though sung Masses had still to be in Latin. It was surprising to see so many of the clergy who had been previously allergic to sung celebrations suddenly insisting that the principal Mass should be sung. A few years later we were allowed to sing Mass in English and one or two settings had come into existence in the meantime to make this possible. For the most part they were not inspiring compositions. Then with the coming of the *Ordo Missae* of 1970 it was apparent to the perceptive that we now had a different liturgical form that suggested a new approach to the singing of the Mass. The emphases were different and the General Instruction to the Missal (no. 19) stated that the ministerial chants and their responses should be given priority over all else. But though we now had new and definitive texts, composers, or most of them, went on writing settings for the *Kyries*, the *Gloria* and the rest as if nothing had happened. Acclamations continued to be muttered by sometimes unwilling congregations and the responsorial psalm, which demands singing, was recited and even sometimes omitted. It was an expendable extra. The ICEL Missal did indeed attempt to provide chants for the ministerial texts but they were broken-backed, the uneasy adaptation of plainsong to the English language – a *mésalliance* if ever there was one. More recently more successful attempts have been made by musicians, who in some quarters are regarded as very *avant-garde*.

Others, not many perhaps, have fallen to a different temptation under, it would seem, the influence of the same ICEL Missal, and have treated the new rite musically as if it were the old. That is, *everything* that was sung in the old rite, including collect and readings, are sung, and celebrant, ministers and choir retire exhausted. Here no attempt was made to ask why we should sing or what we should sing. Epistle and gospel were sung in Latin, so they should be sung in English.

In fact, the first question that has to be asked is why sing at worship at all? Whole books have been written about this subject and I wish to make only one of two simple points.

1) Singing is a profoundly human action. It expresses not merely our emotions but the attitude of our whole human personality to an occasion or an event. We can and do express our attitude or reactions in words, and when these words have the quality of poetry, the expression is all the more adequate to the occasion. When poetry is married to music it gives a completeness of expression that perhaps nothing else can. Here the human person is saying all he can at a given moment, and when the verse and the music are the sort of words and music that are strongly evocative, they say more than we could say by rational discourse and carry us beyond ourselves. Does not St Augustine say somewhere, [1] speaking it would seem of the word *Iubilate*, that the very music can express what we cannot find words for?

These are well known considerations, and if I venture to mention them it is because it does not seem to be generally realised that, if the content of our worship is divine, a content indeed that cannot be encapsulated in either words or music, worship is also a profoundly human activity. It engages or should engage the whole of our personality, thoughts, desires, senses, gestures and actions. This as human beings is how we work or rather, how we

1. *Enarret. in psalmos*, ps.32, *Serm.* 1; Office of St Cecily, Nov. 22.

realise what we are, and when people, for whatever reason, are inhibited from thus expressing themselves, they are to that extent dehumanised. Perhaps the era of the English public school boy, with his stiff upper lip (which makes singing impossible anyway) has gone but there still seem to be some people about for whom singing at Mass is rather like undressing in public. The process of dehumanisation has perhaps gone further than we think.

2) The second observation is suggested by another phrase of St Augustine: *cantare amantis est;*[2] it is the lover who sings. And he does so because his whole being is filled with the thought of his beloved, filled with admiration or even adoration. He is experiencing that movement from self to other that we inadequately call love. To put it more prosaically, song in worship is a sign, or even a sacrament, of our love of God, a delighting in his goodness and beauty, a sign of the movement of self to the Supreme Other to whom we would give ourselves.

But worship of this kind does not just well up from our consciousness – or even from our sub-consciousness – it is not a purely human thing. In worship we are the brothers and sisters of the Risen Christ, it is in and through him that we worship, and as his resur-

2. Quoted in fact in GIRM, no. 19.

rection was for him a moment of unparalleled joy, for he had returned to the Father whence he had come to redeem mankind, so for us when we worship we may share his joy. Of this the church in its earliest days seems to have been conscious; they were visibly one community bound together by love, and their community life, including their worship, was filled with what the New Testament calls exultation or even an ecstatic delight[3].

Always they were conscious that they were united to the Risen Christ as they stood to pray, with gratitude in their hearts, and sang 'psalms and hymns and inspired songs to God' (Colossians 3:16). The source then of our love and joy as we worship is Christ himself, and if that joy is to mark our worship, it is of this in the first place that we need to be aware. It might be said that song in worship is the sign of the Christian who shares the risen life of Christ, just as at the lower level it is a sign of the human-ness that we also share with him.

From this two consequences can be drawn. The first is that if our song is to be of that sort, we must first have grasped something of the goodness and beauty of God, for 'out of the abundance of the heart the mouth speaks'. And how shall we catch a glimpse

---

3. Cf. A. Souter, *A Pocket Lexicon to the Greek New Testament*. s.v. *agalliasis:* 'wild joy, ecstatic delight, exultation'; the last is the word chosen by the Vulgate. JB's 'gratitude' seems to be unjustified.

of the goodness and beauty of God if not through Jesus in whom the fulness of God is to be found, a fulness we share with him who alone has seen the Father and who has made him known (John 1: 16-18)? To know Christ is to know the Father and this knowledge comes in the first place from our prayer, from all we do to cultivate that inner life, the sense of God's presence, which forms the ground base of every Christian life. The quality, the authenticity, of our song will be conditioned by the knowledge of God that we try and cultivate day by day. The second consequence is that our song itself can, and is meant to, lead us to the contemplation of the God who is revealed in Jesus Christ. If our worship is right, if our song is of the right sort, it will create a mood in which we can begin to be aware of the beauty and glory of God. It is not at all easy to achieve this in parish worship where the congregation is so heterogeneous, though a splendid hymn well sung can lift people beyond themselves. Yet plainsong, which in the earlier days of the liturgical movement was so often called sung prayer, was able to do this, at least for monastic communities, and perhaps still does. That may be one reason why ordinary members of parishes seek out such communities, at least from time to time, to share in this mood of contemplation. However that may be, it would seem to follow that whatever composers write

14

for the liturgy, it should have this contemplative dimension or that they should be at least aware that the purpose of their music is to lead people to achieve union with God, whether that be called contemplation or not.

Nor should this be thought to be a limitation or a constriction of composition. We go out from self to God in joy and exultation, in praise and thanksgiving, in sorrow and in quiet meditation, and all these moods can be and have been expressed in the great music of the past. With an adequate understanding of the liturgy this can be done again and to some extent is being done.

The divine and the human, then, those are the fundamental qualities of our worship and they combine – the *imma summis* of the *Exsultet* – to enable man to give himself to God. This is the ultimate source of our song or, to put it another way, in the words of Dame Hildelith, 'Song is for joy – even hidden in sorrow – and joy is praise', so it is fitting that we should sing the liturgy [4].

The Constitution on the Liturgy and the Role of Music
When we turn to the Constitution on the Liturgy we find that it has two things to say which can be described as principles.

4. *Music for Evening Prayer,* (Collins, 1978), p 6.

1) 'Sacred song united to the words (cantus sacer qui *verbis inhaeret*) . . . forms a necessary and integral part of the solemn liturgy.'

2) 'Sacred music has a ministerial function (*munus ministeriale*) in the celebration of the ligurgy' (no. 112).

The first statement is really saying what has been said above, a view that is supported by Father Gelineau in his commentary on the Constitution in 1964:

'Music comes into the liturgy not as an independent element nor as an autonomous art-form. Rather, *it is organically united with the word.* All the signs of Christian worship ought to communicate the revelation of the mystery of Jesus Christ. They cannot be simply the expression of the religious feeling of mankind. The emphasis that the Constitution makes on the mediation of the word echoes one of the major concerns of the whole document which wishes to ensure that the liturgy should have a specifically biblical and Christian quality.'[5]

The word then is of paramount importance and, to give point to his remarks, Gelineau recalls the words of another pope, Urban VIII, who as long ago as the seventeenth century said 'Music is at the service of

5. *La Maison-Dieu*, no. 77, pp. 196-7.

holy scripture and scripture is not at the service of the music; music is the servant of the Mass and the Mass is not the servant of music.' We may add that it is precisely because music is united with the words of the bible and the liturgy that it has a dignity and an importance greater than any other art-form that may be used in the celebration of the liturgy.

Furthermore, if music is an integral part of the liturgy, it follows that a celebration without song is less than complete, and although the Constitution puts the matter rather differently this is what it means:

'Sacred music is to be considered the more holy in proportion as it is more closely connected with the liturgical action, whether it adds delight to prayers, fosters unity of minds or confers greater solemnity upon the sacred rites' (no. 112);

and again:

'Liturgical worship is given a more noble form when the divine offices are celebrated solemnly in song . . . ' (no. 113).

In practice this teaching has been re-inforced in two ways. The *Ordo Missae* of 1970 has to all intents and purposes obliterated the old distinction between Low Mass and High Mass. There may be singing at every Mass and at every kind of Mass, and the General/Instruction (no. 19) strongly recommends that there should be. Secondly, the Divine Office or

the Liturgy of the Hours has been arranged for
choral and communal celebration. There were those
who before the Council were in favour of an office for
the pastoral clergy that would in effect have been a
collection of private prayers and, in this, whether
consciously or unconsciously, they were harking
back to the Breviary of Cardinal Quiñones who attempted to do just that in the sixteenth century. The
Council was more far-seeing and left the door open
for an Office that would not be simply clerical but
one that could be used by the whole people of God.
The Congregation for Worship was not slow to seize
the opportunity and although the new Office is still a
little too complicated, it has been welcomed by both
clergy and laity. It is being used not only by the
former but also by the latter in a way that the Council
Fathers can hardly have imagined.

Since, then, music is so closely related to the
liturgy and in a very particular way to the *word,* it
would seem to follow that music for the liturgy must
be born of a real and deep understanding of the
liturgy, of its nature and shape, of its texts and movements, and of the role that different ministers perform in its celebration.

The second statement is of even greater importance. Music has a *munus ministeriale,* it ministers to
the celebration of the liturgy, it is the servant of the

liturgy, that is, it must serve the over-riding purpose of the liturgy which is nothing less than to draw people into union with God. Positively, it should make the liturgy more real, reinforce its message so that the assembly can grasp it more fully and enter into it more deeply. In particular, as we have seen, it is at the service of the word which, on the one hand, is God's word to his people, and on the other, the people's word to God. Negatively, it should not obscure the shape of the liturgy. There are, as we shall see, certain parts of the liturgy that demand song and often a particular kind of song which will engage the action of the people. Nor must it smudge out the roles of those celebrating the liturgy for, as the Constitution says and as is obvious once the liturgy is understood, not only the president but the people, the choir, as well as others, have a ministerial function to perform in the total celebrations (nos. 26, 28). On this count too then an understanding of the liturgy and especially of its texts and their differing character is necessary for those who would write music for it.

What follows then is an attempt to discover what in the *Mass as it is now* should be sung, and why, and to make some general suggestions as to how various parts should be sung.

A Problem

But before doing that I want to voice a problem. We have inherited a tradition of the Sung Mass that derives from the Latin Mass. There in principle *everything* was sung, only those parts that were the private prayer of the priest being said. The one apparent exception to this was the eucharistic prayer which, however, was probably once sung to something like the simple tone of the preface. For the rest, the 'propers' were always musical texts, that is introit, gradual, *offertorium* and *communio*. With the exception of the gradual all were processional texts and processions demand song. The gradual was meant to be a meditation on the word proclaimed in the lessons and the *Alleluia* a welcome to Christ who made (and makes) himself present in the word of the Gospel. So far, all very comprehensible and functional. Then there was the Ordinary, the *Kyries* – about which there is another problem – the *Gloria,* Creed, *Sanctus* and *Agnus Dei*. These too were conceived to be sung texts and we shall have to say a word about them later on. But in addition to all this, there was the tradition of singing prayers and lessons, and it is these that present the problem mentioned above.

We have inherited the tradition of singing these texts but it seems to be a tradition that derives not simply from a Latin liturgy but from Latin rhetoric. Latin has a quite different dynamism from English and a Latin sentence a quite different rhythm. Within the word there is a clearly defined pattern made up of quantity and accent and as it was originally declaimed, of rise and fall: e.g. *Omnípŏtens, āetérne Déus*. When you declaim it your voice naturally falls into a certain sound pattern which suggests song even if it is of the simplest sort. All the more so is this true of the sentence which is built on the quantities, accentuations, the rhythm and the place of the words. Here is a well known example from one of the masters of Christian rhetoric:

> *Exsúltet sánctus, quia propínquat ad pálmām. Gaúdeat peccátor, quia invitátur ad véniām. Animétur gentílis, quia vocátur ad vítām* (Leo, *Nativ.* I).

That sort of rhetoric, I submit, naturally lends itself to a chant and when the Romans of the fifth or sixth century wished to give full value to words I believe that quite naturally they sang them.

What I am not certain of is whether English lends itself to such treatment. True, we once had the rhetoric of a Milton, a Burke and a Gladstone, though we no longer have anything of the sort. But I doubt whether English rhetoric at its most exalted calls for song as Latin does. The genius of the English language is different. Usually the accent falls on the first syllable: e.g. ápplicable. But even when it does not, the other syllables are uttered without stress or only with the smallest stress, sufficient to make the word intelligible. Thus 'témporary' where the accent is on the first syllable though 'contémporary', has it on the second. When it is used in adverbial form 'contémporarily', the rest of the syllables have to take care of themselves. It is true that this sort of accentuation seems to be becoming obsolete, it would seem under transatlantic influences, so that we get the ugly 'primárily', but in England at any rate the older form is still the correct one. I suggest that this kind of accentual pattern does not naturally lend itself to the kind of cantillation that seems to have been natural in Latin. It does not seem too much to say that if the chants of the old Roman liturgy for lessons and prayers enhanced and reinforced their message, that is, enhanced and reinforced it *for those who heard it*, this is not true of the English language when so used.

No doubt new kinds of cantillation need to be worked out, but before embarking on them it will be as well to ask: should such texts be sung at all? What effect are we aiming at? Are we aiming at anything at all, except perhaps some vague notion of 'solemnity'? But this comes to asking the radical question: *can music exercise its ministerial role here?*

The same sort of questions need to be asked of sung prayers, collects, blessings and the rest. Does a sung prayer help the assembled people to pray better? Does its message go deeper into our minds and hearts? Are we drawn more effectively into the prayer of the president who utters it on our behalf? It is only when these questions have received a convincing answer that we can begin to think about singing texts such as these. What I think is not very intelligent is to sing texts just because they have been sung in the past.

CHAPTER II

The Structure of the Mass

It would be impossible here to consider the structure of the Mass in the way it deserves. The work from the viewpoint of liturgical analysis has in any case already been done by the General Instruction on the Mass in the Roman Missal (chapter II, nos. 7-57). For my purposes here I divide the Mass into four great blocks and examine each in turn.

I. THE INTRODUCTORY RITES

These include everything from the entrance song to the collect. It must be confessed that it is a somewhat miscellaneous collection that offers no clear pattern from a musical point of view. We must take the items one by one. About the *entrance song* or *introit* there is no problem. It is meant to be sung and in its earliest form was a reponsorial psalm, that is, in principle, a popular form, so arranged that the whole assembly could take part in it. There is nothing abstruse about that. It is the most natural thing in the world for an assembly to wish to sing itself into unity.

There are however two problems here. Although

the introits of the great feasts of the year can be seen as integral parts of the Mass-formula of the day, this is not true of the thirty-four Sundays of the year or of the week-day Masses. For these the revisers seem to have taken over from the old Missal the introits that were there with some few additions. I have not made a detailed, book for book, examination but few if any of them seem to have any relevance to the other texts of the day. Nor does the new Missal envisage that they should be sung responsorially. The introit is called *antiphona ad introitum*, and no psalm or even verse of a psalm is given.

What are we to make of them? There seems little to be said for singing them just because they are in the book and as we know their singing is not obligatory. In practice, almost everywhere the Mass begins with a hymn that in well-ordered churches is appropriate to the day, though one fears that in dis-ordered churches it is just a more or less holy noise. One way, then, of tackling the problem is to extend our hymn repertoire so that there will be enough appropriate hymns or songs to cover the whole year. To some extent this has already been done. The hymnal *Praise the Lord Revised* (1973) is notable for its liturgical arrangement and the most recent one *With One Voice* (1979) provides not only a vast quantity of hymns but has a number of new forms (e.g. by Richard Connolly) that make them suitable for liturgical use.

25

For it must be emphasised that if hymns are to be used in the liturgy of the church they must be appropriate both to the service in question, i.e. to the various parts of the Mass and their meaning, and to the day or season of the year. Thus an entrance hymn or song should express the main theme of the Mass that is to follow and a hymn to be sung during the rite of communion should, according to the General Instruction of the Roman Missal, express the sense of unity in those who have received holy communion. As for their form, hymns with a refrain after each stanza that can be easily memorised and so eliminate the need to use a book, are particularly useful for the entrance procession and for that which marks the rite of communion.

If we are dissatisfied with the conventional hymn, is there any other form that would be both suitable and practical? If we thought along the lines of the old introit, we should be faced with the need to sing yet another psalm and, as we know, the existing responsorial psalm is too often not sung because, as it is said, the local church cannot manage it. What is a possibility is that someone, perhaps a group working together, should examine these texts, extract from them what is their essence, look at them again to see if they contribute to the theme of the day and then, if they are appropriate, clothe them in language that at least aspires to poetry. This need not be metrical verse but a kind of rhythmical prose that would suggest cantillation. To this text the people could respond with a phrase or perhaps two that could be metrical and thus easier to learn and sing. Such a pattern would relieve us of the remorseless metrical hymn which, because it is restricted in form, is often restricted in content. Yet at the same time there would be a verbal and musical text that would be within the capacity of an ordinary congregation. Even this would be nothing new: parallels from the Latin liturgy can be found in texts like the *Rorate* and the *Attende, Domine* which however did not strictly belong to the 'official' liturgy.

Another solution that might mark great feasts is to build up the entrance rite into a quasi-dramatic presentation of the main theme of the day. In his highly elaborate Mass for Easter Day, Dr Sherlaw-Johnson has done something of the sort. He has used the verbal text of the liturgy with great freedom (though the message of resurrection comes through clearly), he has combined them with a musical text of considerable complexity that requires all the skill of expert singers, including a cantor, and added a procession of the Paschal Candle that gives movement to the whole rite. There is even dialogue, for the cantor proclaims the Easter message and the singers respond. There is no doubt that this entrance rite is dramatic, though it must be said that it goes far beyond the capacity of a parish community. It is however evidence of what can be done by someone with imagination and the requisite musical skill. Such treatment too of the liturgical texts shows that interesting results can be obtained when we get away from a literalistic interpretation of the words in the book.

There remain the *sign of the cross*, the *greeting* and *the penitential rite*. The first two would seem to be in the category of prayers and readings and whatever solution is found right for them will probably be right here. There may be a stronger case for singing the greeting since this may serve to bring the assembly together, though this has been done by the entrance song. In any case, we have become rather less hieratic in our approach to worship and at this moment the celebrant will want to establish a *rapport* with the people and this he will certainly do in his words introducing the Mass of the day.

The Penitential Rite

Of the three forms the first two do not seem to call for singing. In fact, the singing of the *Confiteor* before communion in the old rite is in itself a counter-indication: it was too highly formalised to become a prayer of repentance for most people.

But in the third form music does seem to have a ministerial role. As is well known, this form combines

28

sentences intended to help the assembly reflect on the compassion of God as shown in the person of Jesus and in the saving works of redemption. These sentences can be varied and ideally should be varied from day to day by the use of texts taken from the Mass-formula or from the season. They can be said or quite effectively sung to a simple chant which may be sung either by the celebrant, a deacon or a cantor. Provided they are well and clearly sung they give the assembly time to reflect on the invitation to repent. But they need to be handled with care and should never be elaborate.

The little problem with the *Kyries* is that people seem to have forgotten their original purpose. They were the common response to a litany – as they are still in eastern rites – whose content could be very various. They do not then necessarily suggest repentance, though in the old liturgy the muscial settings often suggested that they did, and many of the Masses composed in recent years make the same suggestion. This misunderstanding has limited the use of the *Kyries* in the West, though the Divine Office (which has turned them into English) uses them occasionally in the intercessions and there are churches that use them as the response to the invitations of the Prayers of the Faithful. If the *Kyries* do not of themselves suggest repentance, but rather humble petition in the presence of God, they yet have a certain urgency that makes them suitable for use in the third form of the penitential rite. But it needs to be emphasised that they are the people's response and consequently any musical setting that excludes their response is inappropriate. On the other hand, the response need not exclude the choir. Provided there is a strong melodic line for the people to sing, it can be enriched by harmonies which can be sung by the choir.[1] Here then is another interesting opportunity for composers to which perhaps not sufficient notice has yet been given. In this form of the penitential rite music can perform a ministerial function in leading the people more deeply into repentance.

The Gloria

When we come to the *Gloria* we are faced with the question of its literary genre. It is a not unimportant question for if that can be agreed upon, it will condition the kind of music that should go with it. Clearly it is a lyrical piece and a lyric, according to the Concise O.E.D., is a text 'for the lyre, meant to be sung' and usually of 'no great length'. So far so good, but if we look at it more closely we shall see that the first part of it is a series of acclamations: 'Glory to God . . . We worship you . . . We give you thanks . . . We praise you for your glory'. The second part is

1. For an example see *Amen Alleluia*, ed. Margaret Daly, (Veritas Publications, 1978), p. 11.

petition: 'Lamb of God, you take away the sin of the world . . . '. The third part, which is also the conclusion, returns to acclamation. Although I am no musician and cannot say how it ought to be done, it seems to me that the literary genre of this text ought to be respected when composers are writing a setting for it. This may well provide difficulties but one thing I think must be said and that is that the 'through-composition' of a Haydn or a Mozart, not to mention lesser mortals, is contra-indicated. There has, I believe, been some appreciation of the literary genre of this text among some recent composers but the matter needs to be carried further. How are acclamations to be expressed musically? Is a single line melody the right solution? Are repetitions of certain phrases to be excluded: e.g. 'we worship you . . . we give you thanks . . . '? Cannot an anitphonal pattern be properly used here so that the people can have their part in it? Although it is to be regretted that the ICET text has changed the pattern of these acclamations which seemed to rise from 'we praise you' to 'we give you thanks for your great glory' which in itself would seem to suggest a rising musical phrase and an increasing richness of treatment, there would seem to be no reason why this should not still be done musically. Here music should be performing its ministerial role in bringing emphasis and excitement (why not?) to a text that demands it.

The middle section will, of course, be quieter and the two petitions 'have mercy on us' and 'receive our prayer' can echo each other, as they do in some compositions.[2] The final section will, of course, be given 'acclamation' treatment and end strongly with an Amen that gathers up the whole community.

2. THE MINISTRY OF THE WORD

The appropriateness of singing or not singing prayers or readings has been dealt with above. Here the responsorial psalm and its refrain call for some treatment.

The Responsorial Psalm

There is hardly any need to say that the responsorial psalm, precisely because it is a psalm, i.e. a sung prayer, demands song, and where things are done decently and in order, it is so sung. When it is, it is liturgically one of the most satisfying texts of the Mass. Choir and congregation are appropriately balanced, the response is usually sung by the people without difficulty (though a run-through before Mass is very helpful) and often with enjoyment. What is more, the music ministers here to meditation, assisting the people to ponder on the word that

2. Cf. e.g. Bill Tamblyn, *New Community Mass*, 1975.

has been (and sometimes will be) proclaimed. Every effort should be made to make possible the singing of this psalm even in small communities.

The above description assumes a unison treatment of the texts, the choir singing the response which is repeated by the people and then going on to sing the verses in one or other of the non-harmonised settings that already exist. But there is also an opportunity here for a kind of composition that still seems to be somewhat rare, at least in this country. There is no reason why the verses of the psalm should not be sung in harmony by the choir, the people responding in unison with the response. This would give an interest that is sometimes lacking and provide the choir with an opportunity to sing a text that is organically related to the liturgy of the day. It has also been argued, by Lucien Deiss I think, that a more varied approach to settings for this psalm would leave the way open for music that would more adequately express its literary form than the single line melody does. Some psalms are glad, some are sad, and the different moods of the psalms could and should, some say, find musical expression. Not all are agreed about this and some would maintain that in the liturgy a certain objectivity that a single melodic line provides is preferable. This musical form can indeed express the sentiments of a psalm as the settings put out several years ago for Holy Week and notably for Good Friday showed.[3] There is however the Allegri *Miserere,* an example (though not a model) showing what can be done with a rich and elaborate setting. In any case both kinds of setting can and should exist together even if the more elaborate kind will be possible and perhaps appropriate only where there is a fully trained choir and then on the occasion of the greater feasts and seasons of the year

Since the responsorial psalm should be sung at least at every Sunday Mass we need means to secure this. Here what we need is not so much music as people, that is, the trained cantor or leader who will sing the verses of the psalm and lead the people in the singing of the response.[4] Although the matter has been discussed and even recommended for years, little has been done to train such people.

The Alleluia
This is one of the principal acclamations of the whole Mass. It welcomes Christ who makes himself present in his word, the gospel. It deserves the best musical treatment possible.

3. From the St Thomas More Centre for Pastoral Liturgy and more recently in its book *By Your Cross and Resurrection: Celebrating Holy Week* (9/11 Henry Rd., London. N4 2LH).

4. A welcome addition to the music available is *A Responsorial Psalm Book,* edited by Geoffrey Boulton Smith (Collins, 1980) which contains settings for all the Sundays of the three year Lectionary cycle.

Perhaps then this is the moment to ask what an acclamation is meant to do for the assembly. It is addressed to a divine Person and its purpose is to unite the assembly in a single cry and relate it to that Person. Since it is difficult to do this by merely speaking it, it would seem that, by its nature, it demands song, and this view of the matter is at least suggested by the observation of the General Instruction (no.39) that when the Alleluias are not sung they may be omitted. It would seem to follow then that any musical setting for it should be strong, enveloping and attractive enough to draw everyone into singing it.

How is this to be done? In the *Lectionary* we are offered two Alleluias before the verse and one after it. Psychologically, and I should have thought music-ally speaking, this is a pretty desperate situation. Unless a congregation is being conducted (and that is not a very prayerful thing to do) it is difficult for them to come in quickly enough for the first Alleluia and this may discourage them for the second. In practice, it seems that a threefold Alleluia is being used followed by its (threefold) repetition after the verse. This works. But we may ask, what sort of musical formulas have been found for this acclam-ation? At their best some of the Alleluias in the old gradual with their long *iubila*[5] did something, though

5. See Lewis and Short, *Latin Dictionary*, s.v. where *iubilum* = 'a cry, a shout'!

35

in a highly formalised manner, to express the meaning of the Alleluia, but they no longer speak to ordinary people who have no experience of plainsong
and, in any case, most of them are too difficult. The
one that seems to be used a good deal is the simple,
threefold Easter Alleluia and this people find very
singable. There is also of course the Gelineau
Alleluia that is often used.

This does not however exhaust the possibilities. If
a setting has a strong melodic line that the people can
sing, harmony can be added to it and this will give
richness and strength to the Alleluias, the choir
sustaining the harmonies and the people singing the
melody. This too in practice has been found to work.
Such treatment also adds interest, and if an adequate
procession to the place of the singing of the gospel be
made (and it need not always be in the sanctuary
area), Alleluias treated in this way effectively mark
the importance of the proclamation of the gospel
which is the high point of the ministry of the word.

The Presentation of the Gospel

If the singing of the readings, including the gospel,
does not seem indicated, the same is not true of the
phrases that announce and conclude the gospel. The
first of the two before the gospel is an invitation to
listen: 'The Lord be with you' and the second is to be
seen as a proclamation: 'A Reading from . . . ' which

would be all the more obvious if the phrase ran simply 'The Gospel of our Lord Jesus Christ' for that is what it is, the Good News for the day. Given the nature of these phrases then they may very properly be sung and when they are, they create a silence and a listening attitude on the part of the people.

The phrase after the gospel is certainly an acclamation and one would plead not only that it should be sung but that the chant should be similar in treatment to that of the Alleluia and performing a similar function. There would indeed seem to be no reason why the Alleluia itself should not be repeated here since 'Praise to you . . . ' says almost the same thing as the Hebrew Alleluia ('praise God'). If even further elaboration were desired, it would be possible to choose a sentence, the main sentence, from the gospel and set it to harmony. It could be sung while the gospel book is being carried back to the altar. Music here would be performing its ministerial role of reinforcing the message of the gospel.

The Prayers of the Faithful

These are sung, at least in some places and on certain occasions, though there are obvious difficulties deriving from the different lengths of the texts and from the very various ability to sing of those who undertake them. If song is desirable, it would seem best that the invitations to prayer should be said and the responses, which are in fact the *people's* prayer, sung. The singing of the *Kyries* as responses returns them to their original use though, of course, other responses can and should be used.

The Creed

The literary genre of the creed is that of statement, a profession of faith, which has its origin in the baptismal service. It was not included in the Roman Mass until the eleventh century and has always seemed a little anomalous. There seems to be a certain consensus that it should be said though when it is sung in Latin it more clearly appears as the profession of faith of the whole assembly. However, in whatever language it is sung, its musical form should be of the simplest to enable the whole assembly to take part in singing it. This view has been reiterated recently: 'the creed belongs to the whole liturgical assembly' (*Notitiae*, 148, November, 1978, p. 539).

A practical objection to singing the creed is the sheer time it takes, and in parish circumstances this is a factor that has always to be kept in mind. In certain English-speaking countries, though not in the United Kingdom (except for children's Masses), it is permissible to replace the Nicene Creed with the Apostles' Creed. This in any case would make an acceptable alternative and its text could suggest a new kind of musical treatment.

Some Conclusions

It will have been seen that if these first two parts of the Mass (the introductory rites and the ministry of the word) are viewed in this manner, they offer considerable opportunities for new kinds of composition. Certain texts of the Mass demand song and some of them do not seem to have attracted composers. Different kinds of settings combining the song of the choir with that of the people can also be seen to be feasible. Just as in the old state of affairs it was wrong for the choir to monopolise the singing, so now it is wrong to think that the people have to sing everything and always in unison. The celebration of the Mass is effected by different individuals and groups, all with their proper role, and as the Constitution says, all should be able to perform their role. But it will also have been seen that settings of the Ordinary, *Kyrie, Gloria* . . . no longer constitute 'a sung Mass'. There is much else to do and one could wish that composers would overcome their obsession with these texts and turn their attention to others.

It may be thought that what has been suggested here is altogether too much. The new Mass treated in this fashion would become as burdensome as the old. But not *everything* suggested here need be sung at every Mass. The purpose of the foregoing remarks is to point out that there are opportunities that at present are rarely seen or realised. Further, we need

always to remember the smaller community
whether the parish or the religious community
These should not be deprived of song and they de
serve something better than an unrelieved diet o
sometimes indifferent (and irrelevant) hymns. Fo
such communities texts like the acclamations hav
peculiar importance; a celebration in quite humbl
circumstances can be enriched by the singing o
Alleluias, the responses to the ministerial chants, th
acclamation after the consecration and the grea
Amen at the end of the eucharistic prayer.

In an attempt to sum up, I would say that the tw
longer texts, the *Gloria* and the responsorial psalm
by their nature demand song. Of the others, th
people's responses, the acclamations and the re
sponse of the Prayers of the Faithful should normall
be sung and this can be done without exhausting th
assembly or unduly prolonging the celebration. Bu
for these we need suitable musical texts that do i
fact seem to be slowly emerging but which are stil
too little known. Finally, we need to learn what th
English language requires and is patient of, especi
ally in the matter of cantillation, and then it is to b
hoped that we shall get musical texts that will be
come as familar and attractive as their plainsong
equivalents.

3. THE MINISTRY OF THE EUCHARIST

This breaks down into three parts: the presentation of the gifts, the eucharistic prayer and the administration of holy communion.

The Presentation of the Gifts

This does not present any very great difficulty. If we wish for song at this time, there is a reasonably large collection of hymns that meet the case. If there has been much singing in the first part of the Mass there is a case for silence at this point, silence on the part of the celebrant as well as of the people. According to the rubric the so-called 'offertory prayers' need never be pronounced aloud (O.M. 19, 21). Alternatively, the choir might sing a motet though one would plead that the words should be appropriate and preferably taken from the liturgy of the day. Another alternative would be a quiet voluntary on the organ, a practice that not only gives the organist some (little) scope but can be useful in creating a restful atmosphere.

The Eucharistic Prayer

This falls into a number of parts, the initial dialogue, the so-called Preface, the *Sanctus*, the eucharistic prayer itself, the acclamation after the consecration and the doxology. A word needs to be said about each.

41

To tackle the eucharistic prayer right away, let it be said that it is a proclamation and a thanksgiving, the latter defining the former. The Church is at once proclaiming the saving deeds of God and thanking him for them and for the effects they have had, notably in and through the eucharist itself which is the sacramental re-presentation of the paschal mystery. There is no need to emphasise that it is the most important text of the Mass, but that importance is not to be found simply in the consecration and all that it implies. It is important because in it the church is proclaiming its faith, its praise, its gratitude, even its wonder (cf the *Sanctus*) at the saving deeds of God and by so doing effects the eucharist. As the General Instruction says 'The Eucharistic Prayer . . . is the climax and very heart of the entire celebration' (no.54). It is the *whole* eucharistic prayer from beginning to end that effects the eucharist. It deserves then special attention but unhappily even that does not solve our problem. We have to ask again whether song can exercise here its *munus ministeriale*.

Since it is the climax of the whole celebration it would seem to follow that it should be sung at least on Sundays and special occasions and there is no doubt that when it is sung (well!) in Latin it acquires a certain solemnity, of which the Constitution speaks, and for some the singing of the words of institution is peculiarly impressive. What is not so certain is whether the singing of it in English adds anything to it, for example, reinforcing its message and, what is equally important, helping the people to pray it. This alone is an important consideration of which I have written elsewhere.[6] Can the people pray the eucharistic prayer as it now is? But that apart for the moment, perhaps the reason why the singing of the eucharistic prayer in English seems less than satisfactory is that we lack suitable musical texts, though composers are now turning their attention to them.[7] Perhaps the verbal texts lack charm and it is pretty certain that they were not translated with a view to singing. There may be other reasons, but let us not underestimate the power of a *prayerful* delivery of the eucharistic prayer.

It would be as well however to look at the eucharistic prayer again. It too has certain climaxes or parts that demand song.

The initial dialogue demands song and it can be sung very effectively. As the injunction 'Lift up your hearts' indicates, its purpose is to gather the people together so that they may listen to and ponder on the proclamation of the saving deeds of God. Likewise, the invitation 'Let us give thanks . . . ' and its response 'It is right to give him thanks and praise' are

6. *The Once and Future Liturgy* (Veritas Publications, 1977) p.33-4.
7. See the setting of E.P.1 by Mr Paul Inwood.

43

intended to draw the people into the whole eucharistic action. All this can best be done by song.

Although the Preface is and should be seen as an integral part of the eucharistic prayer, and in the pre-Carolingian liturgy was always regarded as such, it none the less has a special character. The root meaning of *Praefatio*, according to Jungmann, is to speak out before someone in the sense of 'in the presence of' someone, not in the sense of saying something before going on to say something else.[8] From this and from the content of the texts themselves we may deduce that the Preface is *primarily* proclamation, the proclamation of the saving deeds of God effected by his Son, Jesus Christ. Hence the ever repeated phrase in the Preface 'through Christ our Lord'. The history of salvation may indeed be continued in the eucharistic prayer itself, as it often is, but the Preface remains the principal place of proclamation. Combined as it is with praise and thanksgiving it seems to suggest song. A practical advantage is that if a celebrant found it difficult to sustain the singing of the whole prayer, he could probably manage this.

A further indication of the appropriateness of singing the Preface can be found in the *Sanctus* which as well as being the first climax of the eucharistic prayer is also the response of the assembly to the

8. *Missarum Sollemnia*, F.T. t.iii, p. 12.

proclamation of the Good News. God is holy, he is filled with glory and in the Old Testament 'glory' signified a dynamic quality: God is communicating his glory to men that they may share in it: 'Heaven and earth are full of your glory.' As Jungmann has put it, to *eu-aggelion* we respond with *eu-charistia*.[9] By *eucharistia* we appropriate the 'glory' of the Good News.

That the *Sanctus* is lyrical and meant to be sung is beyond dispute and one could wish that it were sung at least at every Sunday Mass. Since it is a high point of the eucharistic prayer and essentially a people's response, musical settings, it would seem, should be of such sort as to lift up the whole assembly in a moment of pure praise and thanksgiving to God. How does music do that? It is not for me to say but one would plead that it should have a certain excitement, something into which the people can pour their praise. Have we forgotten that the Hebrew *Hosanna* means a shout, a shout of welcome, something more even than Hurrah? This suggests a further thought. Since *Hosanna* is a sort of shout, a joyful one, should not that word be repeated, each repetition receiving some musical emphasis? Have we not perhaps got too straight-laced, are we not a little too afraid of letting ourselves go, even musically? Have people been obsessed with the injunction

9. Op. cit. p. 22.

of Pius X that there should be no repetitions, for-getting that he was speaking in a quite different context and had in mind the operatic performances that so much afflicted the liturgy in his time and before him? However these questions are answered, the *Sanctus* undoubtedly offers a challenge to the composer.

When a *Sanctus* setting that is appropriate and of good quality is sung, it has the effect, mentioned above, of creating recollection and silence when it is finished so that the people are more ready to listen to the eucharistic prayer and, one hopes, to pray it.

We come to the acclamations after the consecra-tion. Perhaps a word about their nature will be in place. It should be known that they are derived from the *mysterium fidei* which for many centuries formed part of the words over the wine. And the *mysterium fidei* does not refer simply to the Real Presence; it refers to the *mysterium* that is enacted in the eucharist, namely the *anamnesis* or recalling into the present of the paschal mystery. Both these elements are re-called in the acclamations that spell out that laconic phrase, as is clear from an examination of the first three. In passing, may one not congratulate the ICEL translators who have turned the prosy Latin into something like verse? But it should be noted too that they have turned the three Latin acclamations into four and the numbers attached to them in the

English missal do not refer to the eucharistic prayers. Any one of them can be used for any one of the eucharistic prayers and this has a practical import. If they are sung, as they should be, it is not helpful to a congregation to have to sing a different one each successive Sunday – or other days for that matter. One acclamation can be used over a period of time and an examination of the different acclamations suggests that the first is appropriate to Eastertide, the second to Advent and Holy Week and the third – this can only be used if the whole assembly receive communion from the chalice. If that is done it can be appropriately used in Lent. The fourth is the weakest of the four because it is not really anamnesiac, if the word be allowed.

These acclamations, by their nature, call for song and of course the song of the people. They are the second high point of the eucharistic prayer. They seem to demand some musical richness and excitement with a rising phrase, especially in the last phrase of the last two: 'will come again in glory', 'will come again'. They are announcing the great *parousia* which, according to the New Testament, is to be looked forward to with glad expectation. This should be apparent in the music. Again, one could wish that these acclamations were sung at every Mass, at least at those with an assembly of some size. They can add interest and, I believe, prayerfulness to the celebration.

The doxology is another text that demands song and it is one that should be sung at all Masses where that is feasible. It gathers up the whole movement of the eucharistic prayer and offers praise and thanks to the Father through the Son in the Holy Spirit which is the basic theological pattern of the eucharistic prayer. Since it is a ministerial chant it needs a setting that can be sung without difficulty by celebrants of average musical skill but one that does something to express the importance of the words. There is also a practical matter here. Many quite unlawfully are encouraging the people to say the doxology with the celebrant because, as they affirm, the people cannot make much of a single Amen. It is a practice that should be resisted and has come in, I believe, because the doxology is so seldom sung. Further, if the *Sanctus* and the acclamations were regularly sung, the other plea that this text is needed to give the people a greater part in the eucharistic prayer would be removed. Whether we like it or not, it is a part of the eucharistic prayer which belongs to the president of the assembly.

But the Amen also needs to be looked at. I suppose it is the influence of plainsong that has made so many think that four or five notes for the Amen are musically adequate. They are certainly not psychologically adequate because a whole congregation finds it difficult to come alive in a split second and sing the

Amen with one voice, as they should. It is the *people's* assent to the whole eucharistic action that has preceded it, not just a punctuation mark. A threefold Amen in rising phrases with underlying harmony is one way of setting it and in practice it serves very well.

Over all, if the dialogue, the *Sanctus,* the acclamation and the doxology with its Amen are duly marked with song we seem to have a satisfactory liturgical and musical pattern that does much to help people to pray the eucharistic prayer.

4. THE ADMINISTRATION OF HOLY COMMUNION

One of the virtues of the new Order is that it has clearly marked off the communion rite from the eucharistic prayer. It has its own pattern and suggests musical treatment in three different places, the Lord's prayer with its embolism and doxology, the *Agnus Dei* and the communion procession.

The Lord's Prayer

There seems to be a consensus that this should be sung and this is widely done. Music seems to be performing its ministerial role in that it adds solemnity to those all-important words and serves to bind the community together. There are already a number of settings, some better than others, and what we need is a musical text that is good enough to become at least a national chant that can be sung in all the churches of the country. It should be remarked in passing that the invitatory need not always be in the words set down in the Missal, and when chants are set for it due notice should be taken of the possibility of variant texts.

Once the Lord's prayer is sung, it seems right to sing the embolism which should continue the chant of the prayer and end with a doxology of some vigour that will draw the people into singing it.

The Agnus Dei

This text was introduced by Pope Sergius I about the end of the seventh century to 'cover' the breaking of the bread which could be prolonged. In form it is really a litany and as we know from the regulations of the new Missal (GIRM, no.56, e), it may be repeated as long as is necessary, that is as long as there is bread to break. Alas, most often there is no bread to break except the large host used by the celebrant.

But since it is a litany there is no need for the assembly to sing the whole text, as is most frequently done. They may sing the responses 'Have mercy on us' and 'Grant us peace'. This leaves the choir the chance to sing something more elaborate for the first part while at the same time supporting the people in their response.

The Communion Procession

The words of the General Instruction (no.56, h, i.) are formal and clear. First, the action is a procession, a procession of the people who should walk in orderly fashion to the altar. Secondly, it is to be accompanied by song. Thirdly, 'its purpose is to express the spiritual union of the communicants by the union of their voices, to show forth their joy and to make clear that the Communion Procession is a fraternal occasion'. Song here then is very clearly a sign of union, we may indeed say communion between the members of the worshipping community. The role of song at this point is undoubtedly ministerial. But the General Instruction also allows of various ways of producing this union. It suggests that the communion antiphon, as given in the Missal, may be sung, with or without psalm. An examination of these texts would, from a musical point of view, be worthwhile. Many indeed come from the former Missal but alternatives are also given and it is these particularly that deserve attention. Like the antiphons of the old Missal, at least for the greater feasts, these antiphons are usually taken from the gospel of the day. This suggests that they could be used as refrains while yet other phrases of the gospel are sung. Such a procedure would emphasise the truth, so well seen in former times, that the Christ who is present in the word of the gospel is now sacramentally present in

51

the eucharist. If this procedure were adopted it would do much to give coherence to the Mass-formula of the day and help people to see that it is not a series of diconnected texts.

There are of course practical difficulties. A different text every Sunday might tax the abilities of both choir and people who, one assumes, have already done a good deal of singing. However, there are high points of the year when such a treatment would be very appropriate.

Other forms however are possible and allowed and the one usually resorted to is the hymn. In the circumstances of parish worship this is undoubtedly the most convenient, though the restricted number and the quality of the hymns used at this time limits their effectiveness. So many of the 'traditional' hymns about the Blessed Sacrament are 'Real Presence' hymns which overlook other aspects of the eucharist and fail to suggest that it is the supreme sign of the unity of the Christian people. We need more and better hymns and, among other things, hymns with a refrain repeated after every stanza so that the people do not have to bring a hymn-book to the altar with them.

Another musical form suggested is the motet, and if this is well sung and appropriate in text, it can do much to create an atmosphere of recollection. But the words should be printed on the Mass-sheet, and if the motet is in Latin, a translation should also be appended. This is but another instance of how the new rite allows of various forms of singing at this point, including those that are regarded as traditional. There may be other ways too, for one of the as yet unrealised virtues of the new Order of Mass is that it is very flexible and, once understood, very accommodating.

The Conclusion

Should the blessing be sung? There may well be a case for it. The words are solemn and when said do not seem to make an impact. But where the more solemn forms are used we still need agreeable and not-too-difficult musical forms that can be sung by the average celebrant.

It is possible too that the dismissal should be sung, or when said it often sounds simply dismissive.

COMMUNITY AND CELEBRATION

These, then, are some of the opportunities that the new Order gives to combine music with liturgy. More seems to have been said about opportunities than about difficulties, but that I trust is an emphasis worth making. The main difficulty, it seems, is to find suitable musical forms for the opportunities provided and about these I am not competent to speak. There is one principle however that must always be kept in mind. Whatever kind of music is used for the liturgy should be the servant not only of the liturgy itself, i.e. it should be suitable clothing for particular moments, movements, and texts of the rite, but it should be at the service of the community. It cannot be too often repeated that it is the community that celebrates, that the different members or groups of that community have each their rightful role and the music should not prevent them from performing it. It is for the composer to see that his music helps the community to celebrate the rite.

Nor should it be thought that what has been said in preceding pages is a *programme*, namely that everything there suggested is to be sung at every celebration. If there is one thing that has become clear in practice (the General Instuction has laid down the theory), it is that *community conditions celebration*. What is possible in one assembly is not possible in another. What is possible in a large parish church with a competent choir to lead the congregation is very different from a small country church with no more than a harmonium and a very limited number of singers. What is possible in a large religious community with a good tradition of singing will not be possible in a smaller one where there are only a few to sustain whatever singing is attempted. In the smaller communities however it is of particular importance

54

that their members should understand the shape of the liturgy and so discover where the rite puts an emphasis that can be suitably sung. It seems to me that even in very humble circumstances a celebration can be enhanced by the singing of the ministerial chants, the acclamations and the responsorial psalm even if all else has to be foregone. The psalm may indeed seem to present a difficulty, but if there is but one competent singer in a community, he or she should be able to sing the psalm and lead the rest into the singing of the response. If even this seems to be too much in certain circumstances, a knowledge of the appropriate documents will show that for a season like Advent or Lent the use of one or at the most two psalms, repeated from Sunday to Sunday, is a permitted procedure. Since however the psalm interprets the first and third reading, this procedure should be used sparingly.

Someone then, the leader of the community, needs to assess what the community is capable of and arrange the musical programme accordingly. In the past even the humblest parish communities have aspired to a cathedral type of celebration, and the old rite, as well as a bad tradition, did much to suggest that this was the right direction in which to aspire. Let us hope that such aspirations have gone and that local communities, becoming aware of their potential as well as of their limitations, will gradually construct celebrations that are the expression of what they are. Under the inspiration of the Constitution on the Liturgy we have perhaps begun to discover the virtues of simplicity and to realise, again with the Constitution, that this produces a certain nobility rather different from what was once implied by the word 'solemnity', which was so often a meretricious travesty.

To sum up, let me say that if we are to produce satisfactory celebrations, we need first to understand the rite as a whole and in its respective parts and to try and realise what are their potentialities. Secondly, we need to examine the verbal texts to discern what is their literary form, for this should dictate musical forms. Finally, we need to look at the community that is to celebrate the rite and, within the limits of that community's possibilities, arrange the celebration that will be a manifestation, or, if you like, a sacrament-sign of what that communtiy is, a body of Christians, however small, that is the church, who wish to be lifted up in worship to God and express their union, their *koinonia*, in a love that flows from the same God. It is, I believe, within that context that will be found solutions of the tensions that exist between music and liturgy.

CHAPTER III

The Divine Office or the Liturgy of the Hours

From its origins and by the way it has been formed over the centuries we can see that the Divine Office is both communal and choral. It was always the prayer of a community, however small, the various parts of the prayer being shared by different members or groups of the community. As so many texts indicate, psalms, antiphons, responsories, short responsories and hymns, which by their nature are sung texts, it has always been and is choral. Psalms and hymns are by definition songs and the responsories, which are aids to meditation on the preceding readings, can only perform their function when they are sung. Of course, the Office cannot always be sung, or not all of it in a single day and sometimes, alas, it has to be said alone. But let not these facts inhibit our understanding of the Office as it is intended to be and as it is in itself. It is a great pity that what happened to the Mass, which for so many became in practice a said Mass, should have happened to the Office through a development that was never planned. The whole of the Office, which was in fact a monastic Office, first elaborated in the West in the basilicas of Rome, was imposed on the clergy who as the centuries went on, had more and more to live alone. Furthermore, the fact that the Office was in Latin (and the retention of Latin for it after the Council of Trent was less comprehensible and less excusable) made it very difficult for the clergy to celebrate even parts of it with the laity. Private recitation of the Office, which is now a practice that is centuries old, has marked the diocesan priest's attitude to the Office. With considerable equanimity he recites the public prayer of the church in private. The new Office has delivered him from the need to say certain choral texts like responsories, though hymns are still insisted on, but the Office he has to use remains choral and communal.

However, there are encouraging signs of change which have been prompted by the new Office. The change from Latin to English and an improved structure have helped both clergy and laity to realise that the Office is a valuable form of prayer, and here and there in parishes and elsewhere small groups of people, with or without the clergy, are coming together to celebrate it. In monastic circles and among religious of all kinds there has been a considerable revival of interest in the manner of celebrating the Office, and for these reasons it is not unimportant that with the revival should go an understanding of the structure of the Office so that the more important parts can be isolated from the less important, and those parts that demand song should, in fact, be sung wherever and whenever that is possible.

One general principle can be stated quite simply and is in fact the teaching of the Constitution on the Liturgy (no. 89a.) and the General Instruction attached to the Liturgy of the Hours (nos. 37, 40.): Lauds and Vespers (or Morning and Evening Prayer) are the two most important Offices of the day and are described as 'the hinges on which the daily Office turns'. These then must have priority and since they are so important it is they that should be 'solemnised' in whatever way possible. Thus, although Compline, Night Prayer, still makes a strong appeal to many of the laity and although Evening Prayer is rather more complicated, people should be encouraged to recite this Office in preference to Night Prayer. It reflects the pattern of the Christian week (the Saturday-Sunday Office is a celebration of the paschal mystery) and the seasons of the year in a way that Night Prayer cannot. Happily the Offices of Morning and Evening Prayer are available in the book so named published by Messrs Collins (1976). But even within these Offices there are parts that are more important than others, there are those that demand or suggest singing, and it is as well that they should be understood for what they are.

Psalms and Antiphons

The whole of the Divine Office is built round the
psalter, whether a greater or lesser quantity of
psalms is used, and psalms are by definition songs.
The Oxford Concise English Dictionary can describe
a psalm simply as '(a) sacred song, hymn'. Often
enough this is made explicit. thus we find

'Come, ring out our joy to the Lord
hail the rock who saves us.
Let us come before him, giving thanks
with songs let us hail the Lord'

ps 94 (95)

or

'O sing a new song to the Lord
sing to the Lord all the earth.
O sing to the Lord, bless his name'

ps 97 (98).

This in itself is enough to justify the statement that
the office is by nature choral. The matter is so
obvious as to need no further elaboration. The only
difficulty is how best to sing psalms.

In recent years a number of formulas have been
devised of which the best known is that of Père
Gelineau, in the form that has become very familiar
in some English-speaking lands as the Grail Psalter.
For the most part however the psalms of this psalter
envisage a responsorial kind of singing and that is not
always appropriate to the psalms of the Office. At

least that seems to be the case, though here we are brought up against a problem. Since the seventh century[1] in the West what is called antiphonal singing of the psalms, whereby one half of the choir 'answers' the other, has been the tradition and we need to ask whether this is the only way to sing them in the office or the best way. It cannot be the only way for not only was responsorial singing long in use before the seventh century but we have learnt by experience from the Mass that it can be a perfectly acceptable way of singing psalms. There are some however who feel that the continual repetition of the response leads to monotony and in any case they like to sing the words of the psalms themselves. Nor should we undervalue the long experience of the antiphonal form of singing by monastic choirs which has proved in the course of centuries to be conducive to contemplation. The calm and regular alternation of the verses produces just sufficient pauses to make possible the praying of the psalms. We are not however faced with a dilemma. Both methods can be used, and if the literary forms of the psalms so indicate, both in the same Office. Some psalms, for example psalm 135 (136), by their very form suggest a responsorial treatment and yet they appear with others that do not. In practice such variety of musical forms can bring a certain liveliness to the praying of the Office.

1. See *L'Eglise en Prière* (1961) p.823.

This country is not without settings that meet these needs. There are those of Dom Laurence Bévenot and those that have been devised by the monks of Mount St Bernard Abbey which without being 'translations' of the plainsong to English words are evidently inspired by it. As experience shows, a quite ordinary congregation can sing these melodies without difficulty. There are, as I have said, the now well-known Gelineau settings which can be used in the Office, though they are not always as easy to sing as they may seem. Finally, there are settings of the antiphons and psalms for Evening Prayer for Sundays and the principal feasts of the year, edited by Dame Hildelith Cumming of Stanbrook.[2]

No doubt there are others too, and all this means that a number of composers have seen the possibilities presented by the Office in English and are on the way to realising those possibilities.

What then of the antiphons? There is no doubt that, pastorally speaking, they present something of a difficulty. If people can be taught to sing the simpler kind of psalm tone, the same is not true of antiphons. But first let us look at what the General Instruction to the Liturgy of the Hours has to say about them and see whether they are worth taking trouble with:

2. *Music for Evening Prayer*, Collins, 1978.

'Even when the Liturgy of the Hours is not sung, each psalm has its own antiphon which is also to be said in individual recitation. The antiphons help to illustrate the literary character of the psalm; turn the psalm into personal prayer; place in better light a phrase worthy of attention which may otherwise be missed; give special colour to a psalm in differing circumstances; while excluding arbitrary accommodations, help considerably in the typological and festive interpreting of the psalms; and make more attractive and varied the recitation of the psalms' (113).

Evidently then they are to be regarded as important and no doubt it could be said that antiphons at one time or another do all these thing. But sometimes they do not. For instance, the second psalm for the first week of Sunday Vesper I is a psalm of anguish 'With all my voice I cry to the Lord . . . ' and yet the antiphon for Advent is a joyful text that seems quite out of key with the psalm:

'Behold the Lord will come, and all his holy ones with him. On that day a great light will appear, alleluia'.

No doubt an 'accommodation' could be made: when we are in the depths of distress the Lord will come and shed light on our condition. But does it not come near to the 'arbitrary accommodation' of which the

General Instruction speaks? And musically speaking, should not the antiphon express joy and expectation and would it not be in too sharp a contrast to the mood of the psalm? These matters are arguable, I know, but this is not the only example of a lack of coherence between psalm and antiphon. What seems to have happened is that some of the old and traditional antiphons have been retained and attached to a psalter that has a very different arrangement from the old one.

Yet it must be said that antiphons can give special colour to a psalm in differing circumstances, and usually serve to turn the psalm into a *Christian* prayer. Moreover they often help considerably to an understanding of the typological and festive interpretation of the psalms, especially on the greater feasts. The Office would no doubt be the poorer without them and it is part of the genius of the Divine Office that psalms have been chosen (and St Benedict seems to have been the first to do it) that are appropriate to hours and seasons.[3] Where there are so many it is perhaps not surprising that they do not always perform the function for which they are intended and at times seem superfluous. Thus in the new Office, psalm 144 (145), like every other psalm is

3. This at least for the West. Egeria in the fourth century was much struck by the custom of choosing psalms appropriate to times and occasions in the Jerusalem church.

introduced by the antiphon, a 'title' stating the theme: 'Praise of God's glory' which here is obvious enough, and finally, there is another phrase from Revelation 16:5. For a psalm of the ferial course it seems rather a lot and suggests that perhaps the antiphon is by itself not sufficient. One notes too that where the psalms are proper to a feast (e.g. Christmas and Epiphany) the antiphons only are given. This suggests the conclusion that the best way to use antiphons would be to reserve them for the greater feasts and seasons and leave them for optional use at other times.[4]

It is in fact in the Offices for the greater feasts and seasons of the year (with some exceptions) that the antiphons perform very well their function of giving a particular 'personality' to the psalms and make them apt material for use on these occasions. Many, derived from the old Office, are of considerable beauty though, alas, they are difficult to transfer into English, perhaps because they have a poetic quality and often a rhythm that is proper to the Latin. Examples are the antiphons for Christmas Morning Prayer: *'Quem vidistis, pastores'*, used with psalm 62 (63) which goes on to sing of the longing of the Christian to see what the shepherds had seen. Or there are the famous antiphons for the Feast of Mary,

4. This however is not according to the rules of the General Instruction.

the Mother of God on 1 January which used to be used also on the Presentation of the Lord in the Temple 2 February and are of Greek provenance: '*O admirabile commercium . . .* ' (so difficult to translate!). This, it will be remembered, is followed by '*Quando natus es ineffabiliter . . . sicut pluvia in vellus descendisti*' and '*Rubum quem viderat Moyses . . .* ' which recall and weave into a mosaic so much of the Old Testament which is made to speak of the events of the New. These antiphons and others that seem to come from an age that we slickly call Dark have a contemplative quality and suggest moments of meditation in the course of the Office.

What then are we to say about these and many other antiphons and what should we try to do about them? There are two problems, one verbal and one musical.

What follows is not meant to be a criticism of the versions that are to be found in the *Divine Office*. Great efforts were made to turn them into eloquent English, into texts that could at least be said, and if the translators were not always successful, one has to remember that they had to deal with hundreds of antiphons, not all of which are patient of good translation. This in fact is the first problem that has to be faced. It is unsatisfactory that we should have to be content with the Latin texts or that we should have to face the fact that nothing else can be provided in the future. These antiphons we may be sure were not written down all at once. They bear witness to a long process of gestation that came from a pondering on the bible, the whole of it. Their composers also had the rhythms of plainsong in their minds as they came to set down the words that would go with it. Furthermore, they thought naturally and easily in Latin. These three factors, I believe, made possible the antiphons that were and still are (many of them at least) to be found in the Latin liturgy.

For the future then the first thing that would need to be done is to use these ancient antiphons not so much as examples to copy in literalistic fashion but as the jumping-off ground for the kinds of texts that should naturally emerge from people who think in English. We should need to find a new freedom not only where the words of the Latin liturgy are concerned but also in our use of the bible. The monks and nuns of the Dark Ages were saturated with the bible, they moved about in it as in their own world; they did not thumb through concordances, and their only exegetes were the Fathers of the Church. Often they unconsciously conflated texts[5] and always used them with considerable freedom. Our situation is not as easy. Inevitably we know more about holy scrip-

5. Cf in another area the introit for Advent II.

ture and we should be foolish to neglect the findings of modern exegetes whose work can often throw light on liturgical feasts and texts[6] but the pondering on the sacred text remains a necessity. It is out of such a process that we should be able to find new antiphons, as eloquent one hopes as the old, and that will revitalise those that already exist.

But when all this has been done – and it would be the work of years – there remains the problem of setting antiphons to music and seeing how best they can be used by a community. If, for instance, one thought of metrical versions of the antiphons (and these were to be found in medieval usage), it would not be difficult to find material, as witness the *44 Metrical Psalms and Hymns* (1974) of Michael Hodgetts. There are verses here, in crisp language and well chosen words, and no doubt it would not be difficult to find melodies for them that would be soon learnt and easily remembered. But on reflection I feel that the repetition of such texts, even it only annually, would soon pall. I suspect that the best direction in which to look would be the subtle verse of a poet like T.S. Eliot which in the *Four Quartets* bears all the marks of comtemplation. The sensitive use of words with unobtrusive rhythms would, it seems, be an apt

6. See for instance Michael Cleary, 'Feast of the Lord's Baptism' in *The Ampleforth Journal*, Autumn 1978, Vol. LXXXIII, part iii, pp. 1-10.

style for antiphons and such texts might well suggest the sort of music that should go with them.

This music might be either single line melody or a harmonised setting to be sung by the choir or a special group (the old *schola*). This latter style would of course mean that the congregation would not have to sing the antiphons but, as in other contexts, such a treatment would give the people a few moments repose, and when the antiphon was finished the silence that followed would encourage reflection. There is of course nothing new in such a device. Even if they are not very reposeful, there are the Monteverdi Vespers. But there is also the tradition of the Byzantine office, whether Greek or Russian, which has long and at times very beautiful texts (under various names), some of the less elaborate of which seem to be known by the ordinary people. But the same office (and to some extent the Italian polyphonic tradition) provides us with a warning. In the Byzantine tradition the non-scriptural texts, for all that they are of biblical inspiration, have acquired undue importance and have often ousted the psalms. This would seem to indicate that any elaboration of the antiphons, whether in words or music, must always be restrained and respect the nature of the office.

The question then arises how antiphons, whether in single line melody or harmonised, are to be handled. There is no doubt that in any form antiphons are difficult for a congregation. Experience shows that they can manage to sing psalms but the free rhythm type of setting that antiphons require is beyond them and in any case the provision of books with all the verbal and musical texts is economically impossible. Nor is it clear that antiphons are *people's* texts. They are meant to set the theme of the psalm or reflect that of the feast and can very well be listened to and almost certainly better listened to than sung. It would seem, then, that it is here that the role of the *psalmista* (mentioned in the liturgical documents) or the choir can perform a useful and, as I believe, a necessary function. The *psalmista*, say, will sing the antiphon, all others will listen and there will follow a short silence. Then the same minister will intone the psalm which the people will take up. This device certainly gives a more recollected atmosphere to the singing of the Office and should make it more prayerful. And prayer is the point of the whole exercise! Nor, in this way of doing things, does it seem that the antiphon should predetermine the tone of the psalm as it did in the old antiphoners, though antiphon and psalm should of course be in the same key. If the antiphon were somewhat elaborate it would be sung by choir or schola and would contrast quite satisfactorily with the simplicity of the psalm setting.

Such then are the nature and the possible uses of

the antiphon and it may be useful to remark here that it is not necessary to repeat it *after* the psalm (GILH, no.123). A silence may follow and, if observed, we should be doing what Cassian's monks did in the fifth century when a silence (with a prostration!) followed every psalm.[7]

With the psalms go the canticles of Morning and Evening Prayer. These differ in literary form, some having very long 'verses' and some shorter. That from Wisdom 9, for instance, has 'verses' of eight lines, two of seven and one of four; each of them is a single sentence that can hardly be broken up. Such text does not lend itself to antiphonal singing and in the interim breviary, *The Prayer of the Church*, the editor arranged the text for responsorial treatment. This procedure is still permissible, even for psalms, and will be necessary for canticles with longer 'verses':

'The antiphons in the Psalter are drawn up in such a way that they may be translated into the vernacular and may be repeated after each strophe of the psalm as noted in no.125' (GILH, 114).

The second paragraph merely adds that this may be done especially when 'the literary character' of the psalm indicates it. This is certainly true of most of the

7. In addition, there were psalm-collects, a collection of which is promised in the as yet unpublished fifth volume of the Divine Office.

canticles also. At least in one place, the *Benedicite*, this way of singing the canticle is written into the book. The phrase 'To him be highest glory and praise . . . ' is repeated after each strophe, though it could well be repeated here less often.

Then there is the special case of the canticle from Apocalypse 19 for the Sundays throughout the year, except Lent. The song of the bridal church, this in itself is splendid, though it is to be doubted whether it is the right text for every Sunday. It is a bit too exalted in tone for constant use and one wonders why the revisers did not make greater use of the canticle in I Timothy 3.16,[8] the most succinct statement in the New Testament of the saving work of Christ which is the dominant theme of the week-end Office. In any case the revisers have rather over-done the Alleluias; they have given us sixteen in all, of which eight may be omitted in mere recitation. It is too much; if you *listen* to the text even when only eight Alleluias are recited it sounds bizarre. I know of one setting, that by Margaret Daly in *Amen Alleluia* (Veritas Publications, 1978), adapted, as she says, from chants of the Byzantine Liturgy. Here she has found an attractive musical pattern and has distributed the Alleluias in a way that makes the singing of them both easy and enjoyable. She has also written an attractive setting for the Colossians Canticle (Wednesday Vespers)

8. It occurs in the Epiphany office and in that of the Transfiguration.

which has a similar musical inspiration. These samples at least show that where a composer is willing to look at the verbal texts and has some knowledge of other traditions, musical settings of some interest can be devised. No doubt they need a choir, but the singers at the Irish Institute for Pastoral Liturgy where she works are in fact students who have often had little or no experience of singing anything other than hymns.

Where, as with the Wisdom Canticle, the 'verses' are long, the right approach would seem to be some sort of cantillation suitable to the English language sung by a cantor, the congregation responding with the refrain. No doubt this could be applied to other canticles too and granted the existence of an adequate cantor, they would be easier to sing than a full musical setting. We need to cut our coats according to the cloth available so that even a small community can sing these chants or take their part in doing so. Simple song, when it is apt, can and does lead to the contemplative mood that should, as I have suggested, be a quality of all music used in the liturgy.

Responsories

These are intended to be moments of recollection after the readings. In the new Office they always echo a theme of the preceding reading and clearly indicate that the assembly should ruminate on their content:

'The text of this response, chosen from traditional material or newly composed, is designed to cast new light on the passage just read, to place the reading within the history of salvation, to draw it from the Old Testament into the New, to turn the reading to prayer and contemplation, or finally to offer further variety and beauty' (GILH, no.169).

An examination of the responsories in the new book shows that the responsories have been put together with great care, but as far as I know they are as yet without musical settings. They deserve the attention of musicians though one must be reconciled to the fact that it will take decades before suitable settings can be found for all of them.

Again, inspiration might be found in the responsories of the old Office where, though they were often badly divided, they did illuminate the foregoing readings with some effect. The most notable were those of the Offices of the last three days of Holy Week *('Tenebrae')*. The writers, whoever they were, drew upon all parts of the Bible and produced texts which, when combined with the plainsong and later with the best of the polyphony, did indeed become modes of contemplation. Whether modern writers and composers will ever be able to provide anything comparable must remain for the moment a matter of speculation. There would seem to be a number of stages that would have to be gone through before such texts could be devised. The first is that we need to be delivered from a more or less literalistic kind of translation. As I have observed above, those who created these responsories (as well as the antiphons) were able to use the bible with great freedom and a similar freedom is necessary today. The second stage would thus involve a prolonged meditation on the text of the bible that would produce an almost instinctive understanding of it in all its parts. The third stage would be to find suitable words in which to express that understanding, words that as often as not would echo the biblical text rather than seek to reproduce them literally. Perhaps poets or those gifted with the use of words can help in this part of the process. The final stage would be to find music to express what these newly-minted texts were saying. Ideally, the same person should go through the whole process because I believe that only music born of it would produce the sort of responsory that the Office calls for at this point. Granted that this is a tall order, is there any reason why it should not be attempted?

Then there are the Short Responsories that occur in Morning and Evening Prayer and in Compline. These present us with a thought appropriate to the hour or the season. As is well known, they have repeats and should obviously be divided between cantor and congregation. Here elaboration of any kind is out of the question. All that is important is that the response of the people should be eminently singable and this has been achieved in *Music for Evening Prayer* by Dame Hildelith Cumming and her co-workers. Again, at least one reliable cantor is needed and we ought to be paying much more attention to the training of such people than agonising over choirs which are ever more difficult to maintain.

I note that in *Music for Evening Prayer* settings are given for the responses to the intercessions, with (one is pleased to see) optional harmonisations. There is much to be said for this, especially as they are envisaged for Sundays only. But one has to ask how much an ordinary and probably small congregation can manage musically in a single service? There would seem to be a case here for settings of just one or two responses, the *Kyries* for instance, which would soon become familiar to the people. In the new Office, there is, it seems to me, an excess of variations in the responses of the people in the intercessions, and the petition they voice does not always correspond with the intention given out. In fact, the intercessions are in need of revision.

Hymns

I have left these to the last because it is obvious that they are sung texts, and in this country we have one of the richest collections of hymns in the world. Yet even here not all is well. Rich as our collections may be, they do not provide for all the needs of the Office. According to the General Instruction (GILH, 42) the hymn is intended to express the particular characteristic of each hour or feast, that is, the hymn is to be as objective as the Divine Office itself, summarising, say, the main theme or themes of a feast and, though making an application to life, not addressed in the first place to the individual. I cannot believe that 'Alone with thee, my God' is a proper hymn with which to begin a portion of the public prayer of the church. Perhaps it is a matter of exploring *all* that exists and making a selection that is more adequate than the present hymnary. There is, of course, a new compilation *A Song in Season*[9] and I see that as a beginning. We need new kinds of hymns that will be the expressed reflections of modern Christians on the great mysteries celebrated in the liturgy and we need at least variants from the 'classical' hymnody of the sort that might be called four-square with its predictable rhymes and equally predictable melodies. They may be regarded as bread-and-butter for ordinary consumption but we still need others that are more imaginative in both words and music. No doubt it will be said that this is impracticable. Congregations will not learn new hymns, much less new kinds of hymns. This is just not true, witness the popularity of

9. Collins, 1977.

many of the so-called folk hymns that have swept through our churches. They may be good or bad, they are certainly new and yet people have taken to them. In any case, if there is sufficient interest, and if they are introduced gradually and with some explanation and practice, congregations can be taught new hymns provided the melodies are not too difficult. With religious communities it should be easier to introduce new and different kinds of songs.

The Office of Readings

There is one further matter that may be raised at this point. The Office of Readings, says the General Instruction, is intended 'to present to the people of God, and particularly to those who are consecrated to God in a special way, a more extensive meditation on sacred scripture and on the best writings of the spiritual authors'. Whether or not this Office is practicable for the people of God in parishes must remain highly doubtful. It is not easy even for the pastoral priest to fit it into his day. We may presume then that it is meant particularly for religious communities, as indeed the text says. The only element here that needs discussion from a musical viewpoint is the readings. Generally speaking, I should have thought, they were best read, though there may be a case for a more solemn proclamation, at least of the scripture readings, on the greater feasts.

One of the great losses of our time is the virtual obliteration of the Office of the last three days of Holy Week. Here we had a marvellous combination of words and chant that was deeply moving. It is difficult to think of anything in music that is comparable with the Lamentations of Jeremiah as sung in that Office. The highly formalised chanting of the Hebrew letters Aleph, Beth etc. that come at the beginning of each section was in itself a lament that seemed to express perfectly the grief of the church as it commemorated the sufferings of the Redeemer. These chants of course emerged in a distant past of which we still know very little; they were an art-form that was the creation of ages, most probably the creation of gifted people in communities who were used to pondering on holy scripture. We cannot hope to create anything like them in a few years or even decades, but it is to be hoped that they will not be forgotten and that they will be seen as examples, though not models, of what might one day be done. Although criticism of the current Office is not my primary purpose here, one cannot but regret the elimination of this Office and it is difficult to understand why it might not have been left in the book at least as an alternative to the briefer and much less eloquent Office that has now replaced it.

The Conclusion

There is little to be said here that has not been said before. It seems that the blessing and the dismissal might well be sung on at least more solemn occasions. Even so, Evening Prayer at least ends with something of an anti-climax. The anthems of Our Lady have been removed or seem to have been removed. Perhaps what people do not understand is that what is not obligatory is not forbidden. In my view, the anthems can still be retained and where it is the custom, or was the custom, to make a procession from choir or sanctuary to the shrine of Our Lady, the seasonal anthem could very properly be sung. After the anthem there could be some moments of silence and recollection which the very singing of the anthem promotes.

CHAPTER IV

Praying the Liturgy

It is now a long time since the whole of the liturgy was described as the Church at Prayer.[1] At first sight this might seem an over-simplification and so inadequate to express the whole nature of the liturgy. Does it not consist of *actions*, the eucharistic action, the action of the other sacraments? Are there not gestures and movements? Do we not talk about 'celebrating' the liturgy, a term that implies action? At a deeper level is there not the action upon us of God who communicates his life, his love and indeed himself to us in and through the liturgical action? All this is indeed true, for on the part of human beings all worship is a response to God who by his word has made that response possible.[2] This last consideration reveals the posture of the Christian in worship before God. Whether by gesture or sacramental action or by word we are in an attitude of *asking*. This truth is

---

1. Cf *L'Eglise en Prière*, ed. A.G. Martimort, 1961.
2. For a fuller treatment see the present writer's essay 'A Theology of the Liturgy' in *The Study of Liturgy* (S.P.C.K., 1978), edd. Cheslyn Jones, G. Wainwright, E. Yarnold.

illustrated by two statements of John H. McKenna in his *Eucharist and the Holy Spirit*[3]:

> 'The epiclesis (is) an expression of the fact that God realises the eucharist *for* the assembly, through the *whole* assembly and through the *praying* assembly' (italics author's).

Consequently, he continues, the 'epiclesis attitude is . . . absolutely necessary for the realisation of the eucharist, even when it is not made explicit'. All the eucharist is epicletic, we are in the presence of God, we need God, we need the divine initiative before our eucharist can be brought into effect, we have no power over God. That, roughly, is what an epicletic attitude means and it can only be otherwise translated as prayer. Even the action that the church undertakes in the eucharist is a form of prayer, for the Christian community does this action at the command of Christ and in submission to his will.

What is true of the eucharist is true of the other sacraments. Thus St Thomas Aquinas could say that the sacraments are given for sanctification and divine worship since by our use of them we are witnessing to the greatness and goodness of God which in some measure they reveal.[4] We are handling holy things which eastern Christians call

3. Alcuin Club Collections, No.57; Mayhew-McCrimmon. 1975. p.204.

4. See S.T. III, a.60, a.6 and the present writer's *The Church's Worship* (1964), p.161.

82

'mysteries' that bring us into union with God. His prevenience, his initiative is paramount and we can only approach the mysteries in faith which in its turn is a witness to the reality of their Giver, God. It is for this reason that all the new Orders of the revised liturgy require first the proclamation of God's word, which arouses our faith, and then the sacramental action which is brought alive in us because we are prepared to receive it. Likewise, the rites are made up of prayers so that we can express our faith and devotion to God as we, with the priest, celebrate the sacraments.

Above all, the sacraments and indeed every liturgical action are effected by words without which there would be no sacraments. But more than that, in them words achieve a power and efficacy which is unparalleled elsewhere. Even so, and in spite of the indicative form of some of the sacramental formulas, they remain prayers which call upon God for *his* action, for the intervention which implicitly or explicitly he promised when he gave the sacraments through Christ to the Church. It is not an over-simplification then to say that liturgy is prayer and since prayer is inevitably expressed in words it will be as well to consider them further.

Firstly let us consider the power of words, first in ordinary life and then in the liturgy.

During the course of a day all of us use many

words. Sometimes indeed they are a little more than noises. But if our words remained at that level, we could not be said to have social intercourse with others. We should be hardly human. Our words then can and usually do convey *meaning:* we wish to communicate our thoughts, our plans, our desires, our feelings. Just think of the lover who never declared his love! You would begin to doubt its existence! But sometimes words urge people to *action* and actually get them to act. The purpose of public speeches, including sermons, is to get people to *do* something.

Words then are not just the counters of rational discourse, they are not just addressed simply to people's *minds* but to their whole personalities and if they are to reach into the life of a human being they must have certain qualities. Meaning, yes, there must be, but by words we convey something of ourselves. 'I love you' means that I am offering myself to you. Words are 'incarnations' of my personality, by them I reach out to a relationship to another, by them I can give myself to another and in worship I reach out to union with God. This is what the words of the liturgy are for. The words of holy scripture are addressed to us to call forth from us a response, a response that is not merely a sound but the response of the heart. On the one side the words of holy scripture are 'embodiments' of God, on the other they are the 'embodiments' of ourselves who want to enter into communion with God. In the liturgy we do this through Jesus Christ who is the supreme embodiment (incarnation) of God.[5]

In the liturgy then there are two kinds of words, those that God addresses to us and ours that are addressed to him. These latter we call prayers and they are as necessary a part of the liturgy as God's word addressed to us. For unless we *listen* to his word, take it to ourselves and then express it in words, that is in the words that have been found by human agents as suitable for public worship, we are not celebrating the liturgy. We are rather like those indifferent and detached spectators of whom Pius XI wrote in his letter on Divine Worship in 1928. More forcibly, the prophets of the Old Testament said that worship without prayer, without the engagement of the heart, was an abomination in the sight of God. We might recall, too, some words of the Constitution on the Liturgy: 'In the liturgy God speaks to his people and Christ is still proclaiming his gospel' but also *'the people reply to God by both song and prayer'* (no.33). We could say, no prayer, no worship.

Prayer then, the prayer of the priest-celebrant and the prayer of the people-celebrants, is an essential part of liturgical worship. The question is how we go about it. Some do not find it easy to pray the liturgy at all and others may find it difficult in certain cir-

5. The above two paragraphs are taken, with the permission of the editor, from *Liturgy*, vol. 2, Number 5 (June-July, 1978), pp. 216-7.

cumstances. Part of the reason for the first difficulty is that vocal prayer has had a rather bad press for a very long time. Since about the sixteenth century it has been thought of as rather a second class sort of prayer. *Real* prayer was that which happened in the secrecy of the heart, meditation, mental prayer or whatever else it was called. Writers of 'spiritual' books (and the term is not a happy one) had indeed some difficulty in including vocal prayer in their scheme of things and it is significant that these same writers talked of the liturgy as 'the externals of worship'. Motions were gone through accompanied by certain words because the 'official' worship was like that and imposed by the authority of the church. It had to be done that way and every word indeed had to be said. Such writers missed the whole 'inwardliness' of the liturgy which, as the Constitution says (no.2), is the manifestation of the mystery of Christ, the expression in words and song and gesture of the Christ who is present in word and sacrament. The deepest and the greatest things of the Christian faith are present and (partially) revealed by the liturgy and for that reason it is the centre and summit of all the church's life (cf. no.10). What is true of the liturgy as a whole is true of the worshipper. According to his understanding and grasp of the content – that is, the mystery – of the liturgy he expresses his sentiments in word and song. It is so elementary a thing that it is difficult to understand why it was not always seen. When a child is happy he or she responds spontaneously with song and dance, even if both are very informal. As has been said above, singing is a profoundly human activity and the same must be said of prayer. We need to voice what we have experienced and we can have an experience of the presence of the divine in worship. When people say that such and such a hymn is their favourite, what they mean is that the words and music have 'spoken' to them on some occasion, they have treasured that experience and have not only responded to it at that time but are capable of responding to it with word and song on many subsequent occasions. The words and the song *evoke* a response from them.

How then is this response to be prompted and fostered so that people can pray the liturgy? The Constitution speaks of people coming to the liturgy with right dispositions:

'But in order that the liturgy may be able to produce its full effects, it is necessary that the faithful come to it with proper dispositions, that their minds should be attuned to their voices, and that they should co-operate with divine grace lest they receive it in vain. Pastors of souls must therefore realise that, when the liturgy is celebrated, something more is required than the mere observation of the laws governing valid and licit celebrations: it is their duty also to ensure that the faithful take part fully aware of what they are doing, actively engaged in the rite and enriched by its effects' (no.11).

There are three points here which will be taken in reverse order.

1) The celebration of the liturgy communicates grace from God and this must be received, for it is only when it has been received that the worshipper is able to co-operate with it.

2) The minds of the people must be in tune with their voices. Celebrating the Mass or any other liturgical service is not merely a matter of *saying* certain words. The first requirement is that we should mean what we say. The mind and the heart must be engaged if the words and the saying of the words are to become prayer which is a movement towards God, in the traditional phrase 'the raising of the mind and heart to God', or as St Bonaventure put it, the ascent of the mind to God *(ascensus mentis in Deum)*.

3) What then of the 'proper dispositions' of which the Constitution speaks?

In the light of the first statement, the first requirement is that we should be open to the movement of

God's grace or more specifically, of the Holy Spirit,
in and upon us. When we come to worship we are
coming to open out ourselves, our minds and our
hearts to the movement of God towards us. This in
fact is the purpose of the first part of the Mass, the
introductory rites and the ministry of the word.

If we are to be able to do this we need to approach
an act of worship in a mood of expectancy, in an
attitude of waiting upon God. Here we return to the
epiclesis attitude' though this time it is not referred
to the liturgical structure and texts but to ourselves.
What *God* does for us in worship is infinitely more
important than anything we can do ourselves but we
cannot 'produce the full effects' of the liturgy unless
we are open to him, waiting upon him.

But if this attitude is to be acquired, we need some
moments of recollection, in the traditional phrase we
need to put ourselves in the presence of God. *En
bassant*, it is here that we see the techniques of the
traditional forms of mental prayer join those of liturgical prayer. It is a practice that is customarily observed before the celebration of the Divine Office in
religious communities. Before ever a note is sung or a
word said there is a silence so that the community
can recollect itself and become conscious that it is in
the presence of God. This can and should be done
even in private recitation of the Office. In the circumstances of parish worship, especially before the

busy Masses of a Sunday this may be difficult to
achieve though those who would pray the Mass
would be well advised to arrive in good time and use
the minutes available for recollection. But let not the
silence before the act of penitence and that between
the invitation to pray and the collect be overlooked
even by those who cannot manage to arrive in good
time. Both of these moments provide an opportunity
for recollection.

The foregoing may seem to be a series of counsels
of perfection. Things are not like that in reality.
Many come harassed by the cares of family life, come
with small and restless children, come without reflection or just out of habit. But counsels of perfection are
not just irrelevant advice that may be applicable to
someone else. They are meant to point the way to
better things, and in this case better things and the
necessary thing is that we should pray the liturgy. If
we do not, it becomes a mere performance.

Finally, 'pastors of souls' are urged to attend to
this matter and by word and example they can help
their people towards recollection and prayer so that
their minds may be in tune with their voices as they
celebrate the great mystery of the redeeming Christ.

Granted then some measure of recollection before
Mass, how can it be sustained or renewed in the
course of it. Let us consider the matter first from the

point of view of the congregation and then from that of the celebrant.

The Ministry of the Word

After the sign of the cross and the formal greeting: 'The grace of our Lord Jesus Christ . . .' or one of the other formulas the celebrant or another appointed by him speaks for a few moments of the theme of the day (GIRM, 29). His remarks give people an opportunity to concentrate their thoughts and to reflect on the message of the day. His introduction then moves into the penitential act and before that is uttered there is a silence. This is intended to give the people time to reflect on their own condition in the light of the message and to repent of their sins. Without this reflection the following act of penitence will be no more than verbal.

The *Gloria,* though very familiar, should give no trouble. It is what might be called a strong prayer in which we call upon God using some of his great titles:

'Lord God, heavenly king

almighty God and Father . . .'.

We praise Jesus his Son, our Redeemer, and ask his saving intercession. We return to calling upon God, the Holy One, the Lord, the Most High, upon Jesus Christ and the Holy Spirit. These names should ring in our minds even if we do not pay particular attention to each one of them every time we say or sing the prayer. 'Calling the names of God' is one of the oldest ways of praising him, as so many of the psalms show.

The opening prayer or collect falls into four parts: there is the invitation 'Let us pray', there is in the missal most commonly in use a summary of the intention of the prayer, there is the prayer itself and the people's response Amen. After the invitation, the celebrant in one phrase directs the people's thoughts and there is a silence. Here in fact is a 'filled' silence, not just an awkward pause and it is intended to create silence in the heart. There is no need to formulate 'intentions' – the priest has done that – no need to 'think' words – those will follow in the prayer. It is a moment when we should try and remember that we are in God's presence so that when the celebrant voices the prayer in our name we follow him into prayer. The Amen is our assent to the prayer he has made.

When described in words, all this seems a very elaborate procedure. In reality it is not. All we need is a spirit of recollection.

A silence may be observed after the readings and this is done in some churches. It is however not always easy to achieve, but if it can be observed it provides yet another moment for quiet reflection on the reading or on a phrase of the readings that has struck us while they are being read. This practice takes us back to the custom of the monasteries, to the *lectio divina,* and if we should have any doubt as to its efficacy, we should remember that through the centuries it helped to produce saints.

The Alleluia is, as has been said above, an acclamation that is intended to involve the whole assembly. It is a joyful welcome to Christ who makes himself present in the word of the gospel. Provided the chant used is suitable it is an easy prayer to pray and is an indication that prayer is both a simple thing and does not require many words. Through joining in this sung prayer we come nearer to Christ.

In some places a silence is observed after the homily, and where the community is small and homogeneous this can be done to advantage. One or two points of the homily can become the material for meditation.

The Prayers of the Faithful or the 'Bidding Prayers', if properly used, also provide brief moments of reflection between the intention and the response, i.e. the people's prayer. As Bishop David Konstant's book shows the responses can with advantage be varied.[6] The proper use is for the reader to give out the intention, to make a pause for silence and then lead the people in their prayer. Unfortunately this silence is not always observed and the prayers appear rather like a badly said rosary. But once again, it is not necessary 'to think words' in the silences: all we

6. *Bidding Prayers* (Mayhew-McCrimmor 1976).

need do is direct our attention to God, to become aware that we are praying to him through our Lord Jesus Christ. There is a further silence before the concluding prayer said by the celebrant. Here quite properly we can think of people or causes we wish to pray for.

There may be those who think all these silences in the first part of the Mass are tedious and tiresome. Yet there are many others who feel that the Mass as usually celebrated lacks recollection. Those who feel this way are surely right, once it is accepted that the Mass is *prayer*, not the saying of a given quota of words. The simple devices mentioned here do in fact help people to pray the Mass.

The Ministry of the Eucharist

The first act of this part of the Mass is the preparation of the gifts and since a good deal has been said about this in chapter I there is little need to say much here. The important point of this act is that it is a *sign* of the intention to offer ourselves so that we may be offered through Christ in the eucharistic prayer. So whether there is a song, or a motet by the choir, an organ voluntary or silence we should be in an attitude of self-giving. The words of the hymn, if it is of the right kind, suggest this and if there is silence we can formulate this intention ourselves. A useful clue to the meaning of this act is to be found in the first part of the eucharistic prayer: 'And so, Father, we bring you these gifts'. That has been done and now 'We ask you to make them holy by the power of your Spirit that they may become the body and blood of your Son, our Lord Jesus Christ . . .' (EP III). The self-offering we begin to make during the preparation of the gifts is taken over into the eucharistic prayer and there united with the self-offering of Christ. It is only through him that the offering of ourselves and our life can be acceptable to God.

The Eucharistic Prayer

This is the heart and climax of the whole eucharistic celebration and it is important that we should use it prayerfully.

It should be understood first that this is the supreme prayer of the priest-celebrant, what is called his presidential prayer. He prays it on behalf of the assembly and they have their part in it by their responses to the initial dialogue, by the *Sanctus*, by the acclamation after the consecration and by the Amen at the end of it. In all these ways, as well as by interior attention, they have their part in it, they *take part* in it. Perhaps people need to understand that these vocal acclamations are true prayers even if they do not always stir our emotions. By them the people appropriate to themselves all that is offered to them by the eucharistic action.

In addition to this, it is necessary to acquire an attitude of prayerful listening. If it is true generally, as the Constitution says, that when the church prays and sings, the faith of those taking part is nourished, their minds raised to God, so that they may offer him their reasonable service and more abundantly receive his grace (no.33), it is nowhere more true than in the eucharistic prayer which is the church's prayer to the Father through his Son made in the Holy Spirit. For continued listening the eucharistic prayers may seem rather long though the second is quite short and only the fourth is really long. There may be a case then for using the Missal at this point, but it should be used not simply as *reading* but as an aid to attention and, above all, prayer. But the eucharistic prayers have now become familiar and it should be possible – and it is certainly a much better way – to listen to them so that their words can sink into our minds and prompt a movement of the heart towards God. The acclamations that punctuate the course of the prayer should be seen as moments when prayerful attention can be renewed.

There are four ways by which prayer at the time of holy communion is prompted or fostered. There may be a hymn which, if well chosen, can be a real prayer inviting the worshipper to appropriate the fruits of the sacrament. There may be simply a silence and at

this time there is an opportunity for a more prolonged prayer of a personal kind. In a crowded church
this requires a real effort of concentration and printed prayers for the use at this time, usually found in
Missals, will help concentration though there is no
need to say them all or even to say the whole of a
single prayer. If but one thought is helpful it is best to
stay with that. Thirdly, there may be a motet by the
choir which, if of the right kind, will create an atmosphere of prayer. The same is to be said of the fourth
way, the playing of a voluntary on the organ. Both of
these last may help towards relaxation and for this
bodily posture is also important. It is not irreverent
to sit after communion if it is more helpful to prayer
to do so. But it also needs to be said that this sort of
personal prayer after communion should not exclude
all thought of the community who are receiving the
body and blood of Christ. This is the great sign, the
sacrament-sign of the unity of the whole assembly –
'it is the one bread that makes us one body' – and we
should pray for our fellow-members in the body of
Christ, remembering their needs, their sufferings,
their hopes and their joys.

If efforts of this sort are made, then the concluding
prayer will in fact sum up all our devotion and put
the seal on all we have tried to do and say.

The Use of a Missal

The Missal has once again come to be widely used. There are various reasons for this: people like to have the text available to them; readers are not always as clear as they should be; there may be distractions of one sort or another in church on Sunday morning; there are those who are hard of hearing. The Missal then still has its uses but it is to be regretted that it is tending to prevent people from listening to the spoken word. People who have no need to do so, keep their eyes glued to the printed text and do not really *listen* to what is being read. If the readings are delivered properly they would find that listening is a much more contemplative attitude than reading.

Undoubtedly the best way to use the Missal is to read the texts over the previous night or before Mass, ponder on them for a while and then at Mass simply to listen. This makes it possible to pray with the celebrant and to take in the content of the readings.

Prayer and the Celebrant

Among the various ministers who take part in the celebration of the Mass the priest-celebrant performs a role of unique importance. His importance lies in the fact that not only is he the one indispensible minister who effects the sacramental sacrifice, but in the fact that he is the president of the whole assembly. This role of his is set out clearly in the General

Instruction of the Roman Missal:

'In virtue of his ordination the priest is the member of the community of the faithful who possesses the power to offer the sacrifice in the person of Christ. It is his function therefore *to preside over the community;* it is for him to *lead their prayer,* to proclaim to them the good news of salvation and to associate the people with himself in offering the sacrifice to God the Father through Christ in the Holy Spirit; he distributes to his brethren the Bread of eternal life, and himself receives it with them'. Hence, when he celebrates the eucharist, *'he is to serve God and the people* with dignity and humility, and by his *general behaviour and the manner in which he utters the sacred words he should make the faithful realise the presence of the living Christ'* (no.60).

There is much that deserves attention here. Suffice it to point out the matters that are relevant to our purpose. If he is president it is so that he may lead the people in prayer. It is for him to make that possible for the people. 'He is to serve God and the people'; the Latin here is rather stonger than the English translation: he should *(debet),* almost 'it is his duty', to serve God and the people. While conscious of the presence of God he should realise that *his very celebration of the liturgy is a service of the people.* This is a truth that is not always appreciated. He will serve the people in many other ways but his service of the people in and by the liturgy is of supreme importance because here he is the servant of the holy things entrusted to his ministry and because all his other forms of service can be taken up into the celebration and offered to God. Finally, he is reminded that his bearing *(modo se gerendi)* and the way he utters the words of the liturgy will be a means by which he helps the people to remember that they are in the presence of God. In a word, we could say that by these means he will help them to pray.

These injunctions are no doubt quite demanding and perhaps it will not always be possible for the priest to do full justice to them. Many a priest has to celebrate Mass three times a Sunday, he is some-times harassed by other pastoral cares on the same day, he may be unwell and few people seem to realise that to celebrate Mass as it should be celebrated one needs to be in good health. Nevertheless, if he has a right attitude to celebration he will be able to per-form his role adequately, but the right attitude will come only from a general understanding of his role and an acceptance of it. How he can celebrate so as to lead the people in prayer will be the theme of what follows.

How then can the requirements of the church be met? First and obviously by *preparation*. This is spirit-ual and material.

Spiritual: For the preparation of his homily the priest will have examined and pondered on the readings appointed for the day. He will search out their meaning and their relevance for a particular Sunday or feast day. But some time before Mass he will read over the other texts of the Mass-formula, again seeking out the meaning and becoming familiar with their content. Where there are alternatives (as e.g. the eucharistic prayer) he will decide which is to be used and by one means or another convey to the people information about what texts are to be used. As he looks through the Missal shortly before Mass to see that the markers are in place, he will be able to ponder for a few moments once again on the texts he is going to use. As he considers the various texts, whether of the readings or the prayers, he will frame the remarks he will make as an introduction to the Mass and of any 'interventions' he may make in its course. The commentary or catechesis to be given before the readings should certainly be written out.

The *material preparation* will consist of the following: readers, servers or any other assistants need to know what they have to do; it will have been agreed with the choir what hymns, Mass setting and other chants are to be used. In a well organised church all these preparations are a matter of routine and make no great demands on the priest.

In addition he will see that the vessels, vestments

and anything else required for Mass are prepared. A good sacristan will see to all this though a final check from the celebrant prevents omissions.

The point however of these obvious and perhaps detailed observations is that the celebrant may begin the Mass with *recollection*. This is the condition of a recollected celebration that will lead the people into prayer. Nothing will do this better than the recollected bearing of the celebrant. He knows exactly what he has to do and is intent on the doing of it. He has not got to summon up pious thoughts, he should not cut himself off from the people whom he is there to serve; he utters the words as well and as clearly as possible and is careful to perform all the ritual actions with dignity.

The one result of preparation and recollection is that he will himself be able to *pray* the texts of the Mass instead of merely saying them. By now he will be familiar with the content of the prayers, he will know what they are saying and it will not be necessary for him to have his eyes glued to the text as if he were deciphering an ancient and obscure document. Whether he is delivering a prayer or the gospel of the day, it is a good thing to look at the people from time to time. By this he shows that he is with them, is trying to serve them and desirous of leading them into the prayer or into an understanding of the gospel.

During Celebration

This attitude of recollection needs to be sustained during the whole of the celebration and the church has now provided moments when this may be done. There are certain scheduled silences in the celebration and others that are either a matter of commonsense or optional. The first are the silences before the penitential act, before the opening prayer, at the end of the 'Bidding Prayers' and after communion. These should be observed with care and not perfunctorily. It is precisely at these moments that both priest and people can turn the celebration into prayer, a prayer that is their own and not just something in a book. Too often they are hardly observed at all, to the great detriment of the people's prayer.

Other silences are a matter of commonsense. Where there is a large assembly people need to be given time to sit down or to stand up. Thus readers should be instructed not to begin the reading before the people have sat down and are quiet. After the *Sanctus* when the people kneel, the celebrant should give them time to do so and only then begin the words of the eucharistic prayer. It is distressing to observe that sometimes the first paragraph of the prayer is drowned in the noise of people settling down. The same must be said of the moments before communion, after the *Agnus Dei* has been sung or said. The Missal provides a private prayer for the

celebrant at this time and yet one has noticed celebrants sometimes say this prayer while the choir is
singing the *Agnus Dei* and as soon as it is finished he
begins 'This is the Lamb of God'. Let there be a
pause here while the celebrant says the prayer and
the people have a few moments to recollect themselves.

Finally, there are optional silences, after the readings (and/or homily), during the preparation of the
gifts and after the acclamation after the words of
institution. Of the first kind something has been said
above. Silence during the preparation of the gifts is
often indicated if the people have had a good deal to
sing in the first part of the Mass. As for the third, the
celebrant may make an intervention here but he may
also mark the moment by a short silence that the
sung acclamation will have helped to create.

All these moments of silence give to the whole
celebration an air of calm and make it prayerful.
Nothing is more calculated to turn the celebration
into a stream of words than one that is taken at speed
(if the expression may be allowed) and one text or
event follows immediately after another without in-
termission of any kind. It is that sort of celebration
that people complain of in the columns of the
Catholic press. Nor should it be thought that the
observance of the silences will unduly prolong the
Mass. If all is well prepared, if a prompt start is

made, if the homily is concise and to the point and if
auxiliary ministers are used for the distribution of
holy communion, the whole celebration can be accomplished without haste in about an hour.

The Celebrant and the Eucharistic Prayer

Although it is obvious, what first needs to be emphasised is that the eucharistic prayer is *prayer*. It is
not just a formula, even a prolonged one, for the
'production' of the sacrament. It is a prayer directed
to God asking that *he* will effect in the celebration the
sacramental-sacrifice which the church, the local
assembly, celebrates at the command of his Son (cf.
EP III). Furthermore, through his praying of it the
celebrant is intended to lead the people in prayer, the
prayer of eucharist. Of this a rapid delivery, without
attention to the *meaning* of the words, without observ-
ing the punctuation or the sense lines the translators
have deliberately provided to assist good celebration,
is completely destructive.

What then should he do? If the celebrant has a
certain recollection, if he has a sense of the importance and sacredness of the words, which in the eucharistic prayers are so often the words of holy scripture, he will unconsciously convey to the people that
he is praying and not just reading a text. In addition,
he will observe the material details of punctuation
and the rest, and use a calm and not declamatory

voice. Some celebrants labour under the delusion that the louder they speak the more the message of the text, whatever it is, is going to reach the people. It is not mere sound that is going to help them to pray but a deliberate, calm utterance without false emphases or any kind of ecclesiastical voice. The celebrant must indeed be himself but, whether he likes it or not, he is performing a public function and his words as well as his actions must be suitable to that function. He needs to realise that all he says and does is at the service of the people.

But is not all this attention to detail destructive of his own prayer? Has he got to think of the meaning of *every* word and consciously raise his mind and heart to God in every phrase and gesture of the Mass? This is not necessary, nor is it possible. But if all else is done, as suggested above, if he has an awareness that he is serving God as well as the people, and if he has acquired what I have called a recollected attitude, his celebration will have the qualities of calm and prayerfulness that is desired and necessary.

The Rite of Communion
It is a common complaint that Catholic priests say the Lord's prayer so fast that no one can keep up with them. Where this is done in parish churches, the poor people just trail along after him and the result is a confusion of words that no one could call prayer.

Surely no irreverence is intended, but there seems to be a failure to realise that they are the Lord's own words with which we may address the Father. In the Missal the petitions of the prayer are set out in lines with certain marks of punctuation. If these are observed the speed of the prayer will be slowed down and the people will have time to pray it instead of merely saying it or at worst just stumbling through it.

In administering holy communion there seems to be a particular need for reverence. Reverence towards Christ in the Blessed Sacrament seems to be on the wane. The celebrant, by his attitude at this time, will give an example that others may follow. As he pronounces the words when he holds up the host he should be particularly careful to be recollected and as he gives holy communion he should be unhurried. It does not seem always to be realised by the clergy, who have so much else to do in the celebration of Mass, that this is the great moment for the people. They should be given time to make their communion calmly and devoutly and this is hardly possible when it is given at great speed along the altar rail. The difficulty of numerous communicants can be got over by the use of auxiliary ministers which is a necessity in these circumstances. Fortunately, more and more bishops are giving permission for the institution of such ministers and there is no reason to hang back on the matter.

After communion there may be song or silence. In practice it is usually possible to have both and a few moments of recollection before the conclusion of the Mass seems right and necessary

The whole matter of the celebrant's praying of the Mass may be summed up in some observations of Joseph Gelineau in his book *The Liturgy Today and Tomorrow*.[7] He distinguishes between *reading* prayers and *praying* the prayers of the liturgy. If the celebrant merely reads

> 'he sets a distance betwen himself and his hearers and so makes it difficult for the people to pray (in their hearts) the prayer that belongs to the whole assembly. But if the celebrant has pondered on the text of the prayer and *made it his own* the people will be aware that he is praying and will themselves be led to prayer.'

7. Darton, Longman and Todd, 1978, pp.108-9.

CHAPTER V

Praying and Singing

The purpose of this chapter is to explore the relations between praying and singing. What happens when we sing prayers, hymns, acclamations, prayers like the *Gloria in excelsis* and perhaps the creed, or what should happen? It is probable that most people take the whole matter of sung-prayer for granted. This is almost certainly the case when we sing conventional hymns: people sing them quite naturally, never asking themselves whether they are praying at the same time. They just do not analyse what they are doing and in this case there is no reason why they should. At best words and melody in these hymns are so fused that it is difficult to think of them apart. Evidence of this can be seen when a new tune, which may be a better tune, is suggested for a hymn that has long been associated with another. But there is the danger that people do not at times pray when they sing hymns; the words remain unexamined, the tune carries them on and all is done without reflection. The rendering of the hymn has become mechanical and although it is agreed that a good tune can 'carry' poor words, we can conclude that words do very much matter. The better the words, the better the hymn *as prayer*.

If the combination of prayer and song is not difficult and is perhaps normal with hymns, other texts, consisting of a greater quantity of words, or words that are less familiar and set to melodies that are unfamiliar or more complicated, offer greater difficulties. Should we attend primarily to the words? Or to the music? And if we do the one or the other are we praying? Is it not possible to see in this attention a barrier to *real* prayer which ought to be conscious of God at all times? In an attempt to find answers to these questions it may help if we consider briefly different kinds of prayer.

It is possible to identify three kinds of prayer. There is the silent prayer of the heart, the kind of prayer that is necessary for the Christian life of all of us if we are not to become superficial and out of touch with God. There is vocal prayer which is also important first because it is the external expression of the sentiments of our mind and heart and secondly because most of the liturgy consists of it. There is, thirdly, sung prayer that is vocal prayer combined with song. This, obviously, is an extension or particular form of vocal prayer and is an expression of prayer that, from time to time, as we have seen often enough in this book, *demands* song. Yet there are those who do not like it overmuch or perhaps not at all. It distracts them, they say, from their prayers or more particularly from the prayer of the heart. This view implies that there is only one genuine form of prayer, which is private and interior. If this were so, public worship would be an irrelevant intrusion into the life of the Christian and were better done away with altogether. Put like that, no one is prepared to accept so drastic a consequence. Why then do people think like this?

The first reason is that they have a wholly inadequate understanding of public worship. They wish to pray, or say their (own) prayers *on the occasion* of the public prayer of the church which logically they must indeed regard as irrelevant to themselves and their needs. The second reason is that they think they have always got to be reflecting on their own thoughts and have to be formulating 'mental' words, intentions, resolutions, petitions and what not. Even in private prayer it is difficult to maintain that degree of intensity for any length of time, and with the 'distractions' of public worship one would have thought it impossible. But this sort of prayer is also often (though unconsciously) egocentric and fails to take the person praying out from self to God who is the supreme object of prayer and on whom the liturgy is inexorably centred. Through the whole of its manifold action, by prayer, by readings, by symbols and gestures, we are giving ourselves to God through Jesus Christ our Lord.

With egocentricity goes naturally a lack of sense of community that was born of the old way of celebrating the Mass. The rubrics to the contrary notwithstanding, it was often all but silent, the priest got on with *his* business at the altar, the people with theirs in the pews, and their business was often prayers read or said from books of private devotion. Even those who in more recent time 'followed the Mass with a Missal' did not always realise that their liturgical service was parallel to rather than part of what was happening at the altar. Whether we like it or not, the Mass, all the liturgy, is public worship that can be public worship only when it is celebrated by a community. As the Constitution on the Liturgy says 'Liturgical services are not private functions, but the celebrations of the Church, which is the "sacrament of unity" – namely the holy people united and ordered under their bishops' (no.26). Song is a sign of that unity and an effective sign, for it brings about unity of mind and heart and binds a community together so that it realises that it is one people (cf. CL no.112 and GIRM no.56, i: 'Fosters unity of minds').

The extreme devotional individualism of the past five centuries is largely responsible for these attitudes. Prayer was regarded as so private that even husband and wife often found it difficult to share their prayers and the horizontal relationship that exists between the members of the worshipping community was something to be feared or rejected. There was and still is a failure to realise that in the liturgy it is the community, united by Christ himself, that gives worship to God. But there is another factor. Catholics for many decades now have, for the most part, attended only the Mass and have tried to cram into their 'assistance' at it most of their devotional habits and practices. Such a way of using the Mass just will not work. Except for holy communion the Mass as such has to be neglected: the readings are distractions and the prayers are those of someone else. Yet private prayer is, as we have said, a necessity and it is a pity that people do not realise that they can pray during the week in church, or at home. In fact, considerable numbers of Christians who find the present liturgical situation very satisfactory are doing precisely that, praying parts of the Divine Office, reading the scriptures and in the busy atmosphere of family life creating periods of recollection. Nor do the retreat houses and conference centres lack clients and the charismatic movement has brought about a real spiritual renewal for many. The spiritual renewal, thus acquired, can and should enrich the celebrations of the worshipping community which, when all is said and done, is a community of people who pray.

Granted then that we have the right attitude to public worship, there remains the question of the relationship between the prayer of the heart and words, viz, vocal prayer, and the further relationship between said prayer and sung prayer. There are two aspects of vocal prayer that need to be taken into account. Because it is a natural thing to do, because, that is, it is a profoundly *human* thing to do, mankind throughout the ages has 'vocalised' or expressed its interior sentiments concerning God and its relationships with him. This is true of even the most interior prayer and the saints and mystics have felt impelled to give expression to what they have experienced or found in prayer. When they have written down their prayers or experiences these have been found helpful to others who have repeated such words. Prayer then, even humble prayer, is the expression of our experience of God, and if the connection between the experience and the words is lost or overlooked, vocal prayer becomes mechanical, almost automatic.

In the liturgy however there are prayers that have been devised and written by others than ourselves. Or rather, throughout the ages the praying community that is the church has evolved certain kinds of expression that are adequate (as far as can be) for speaking to God and suitable for the worship of a community. To mention no others, the prayers of the Roman liturgy at their best give deep and broad

114

insights into the nature of God and of his dealings with mankind. Directed to the Father, they are profoundly Christocentric and make us concious that we are always praying through Christ in the Holy Spirit. It is easy to forget this all-embracing pattern of Christian prayer and we do so to our spiritual detriment. The second aspect of vocal prayer, then, when it is that of liturgy, is that it suggests to us thoughts and desires and intentions that extend our understanding of prayer itself. These thoughts, desires and intentions we need to make our own and it is one of the virtues of the current liturgy that it makes this possible at all the great moments of the liturgical celebration.

So the words of others can become our words, the words of the brothers and sisters of Christ who make up the worshipping community. The connection between meaning, intent and word is thus kept. There is hardly any need to speak of the sense of unity in mind and heart that can be perceived when a Christian community prays in this way.

It is in this context that we can best consider the question of singing or what I have called sung prayer. It is here that the importance of the ministerial role of music can be seen. Its role, as we have said above, is to enhance and reinforce the message of the words To this we can add that it should strive to illuminate the meaning of the words so that a sung text is saying *more* than the words could. Contrast for instance the impact of simply *saying* 'Christ for us was made obedient to death . . .' and that of the plainsong *'Christus factus est pro nobis . . .'.* This grave and lovely melody spoke to the heart in a way mere words could not. From the point of view of prayer, song has a similar function to that of vocal prayer. It comes from outside us, helps us to an expression of our worship that we could not otherwise achieve and gives a dimension to our prayer that is beyond the capacity of most of us. In a word, it is a means, and often a very powerful means, by which we can appropriate the meaning of the liturgical texts. Without wishing to repeat what I have said above in the first chapter, it is important to emphasise once again that if music for the liturgy is to help people to pray, it must be a suitable expression of the literary forms and functions of the texts. When it is, it becomes concorporate with the words and *together with them* expresses the prayer of the community. When this is achieved, the tension between saying and singing is resolved.

There are however at least three different groups in any liturgical assembly whose needs and roles indicate differing approaches to the singing of the liturgy. There are the people, the choir and the ministers who have to sustain an individual role while of course remaining servants of the community. Let us consider the matter from these three different points of view.

The Communiity

Certain texts belong to the community even if they are responsorial, acclamatory or pieces that they may sing throughout.

The third rite of penitence in the Mass is responsorial, the *Kyries* being the responses of the people. They are short, their meaning and function are clear, they do not require any great powers of reflection and song here obviously exercises its ministerial role of giving penitential significance to the phrases expressing repentance. Prayer and song have come together.

Even with the *Gloria* there is no great difficulty. Its general meaning is clear: it is a hymn of praise, thanksgiving and supplication. If the music is appropriate, suitable for singing by the community or arranged so that they can take part in it, it should not be necessary for the people to reflect on every phrase, but if the composer has thought about the text he may bring new insights to its understanding. But basically it is a joyful song and joy is the dominant sentiment that the musical texts should suggest.

With the responsorial psalm the case is a little different. Here it is the words that count. It is intended to help the people to meditate on the message of the day conveyed by the readings and on the verses of the psalm itself. To these they respond with the words that usually encapsulate the theme of the psalm chosen for the day and frequently point on to the gospel. Here then attention to the words is very much in place, but that attention is turned into prayer by the verbal and musical forms themselves. While choir or cantor are singing the verses the people listen and express their prayer in the response. The responsorial psalm is a good example of how listening with vocal participation can be genuine sung prayer.

Of the Alleluia and other acclamations of the Mass I have spoken in the first chapter of this book. Here all it is necessary to say is that they are perhaps the most significant examples of how prayer can fuse with song. The words are of the simplest, the song enhances them (or should do so) to the point where they are seen for what they are: joyful and, one hopes, harmonious shouts to God.

Whether the eucharistic prayer is said or sung, the one thing to be remembered is that it is *prayer*, in the first place the prayer of the president which he pronounces on behalf of the community so as to lead them into prayer. But it is not necessary for the people to say the words, even silently, with him, nor is it necessary that they should read the words unless this helps their attention. With a sense of reverence, with a realisation that 'the work of our redemption' is being accomplished among us, we should listen to the words and let their meaning enter our minds and hearts. This prayerful attention is voiced in the *Sanctus* and the acclamations that punctuate the prayer. It is another case of praying by listening and responding. The length of the eucharistic prayer or a lack of quiet in church may make such attention difficult, but the difficulty is no greater than that presented by any other form of prayer.

The Lord's Prayer is solemn and majestic and yet suppliant, the prayer of the Christian people who are expressing their total dependence on their Father. Song which slows down the speed of utterance helps us to dwell momentarily on the familiar phrases so that we can sing them with meaning and out of a full heart.

Finally, the *Agnus Dei*, whose text offers Christians at least no difficulty, is a plain, straightforward prayer of supplication for forgiveness a few moments before receiving holy communion. Said, the words often pass too quickly; sung, their message penetrates more deeply into the heart.

These are just some examples of how song combined with words can become prayer, examples to show that singing can without difficulty become prayer.

The Choir

The role of the choir is to lead and support the assembly. Consequently it has to be more competent than other members of the assembly precisely because it leads and from time to time has to undertake music that is more difficult. The matter of singing and praying becomes a little more complicated. First, let us recall that the choir performs a ministerial function in the total celebration (cf CL, no.29) and this understanding of their role should dominate their whole action. They are there to serve the community and, as in any act of service, whether it be the nursing of the sick or the feeding of the hungry, we cannot always be reflecting on what we are doing or examining our motives or indeed thinking of ourselves at all. Their task then is to sing whatever they have to sing as well as they possibly can so that they may lead the assembly into prayer, into a response to God. If they are to do this, they need first to understand the texts they have to sing and the function of the texts in the liturgical celebration. Such an understanding will come in the time of rehearsal and it is incumbent upon the choir director to see that the choir do understand and appreciate what they are required to sing. The results of such preparation always appear in the subsequent celebration of the liturgy.

The second point to be made is that the choir has

to give special attention to the right enunciation of the words and the correct rendering of the music. Neglect of either is the recipe for bad singing and that causes irritation on the part of the people and leads them *away* from prayer. But this attention to words and notes, to all the techniques required for good singing, may seem to distract the choir from prayer. If we think of prayer as *exclusively* reflection on words this may seem to us to be so. But first the choir, after rehearsal, will have the general sense of what they are singing and secondly, the correct singing of what is to be sung is part of *their* prayer. They are not just emitting sounds, however beautiful – or not. Moreover worship is fundamentally a giving of self and the choir are giving themselves by their song both to God and to the people they serve. This is simply a long way round of saying that they are exercising a ministerial role to help others to pray. But if they have previously reflected on the texts they will be singing what they mean and the result will be sung prayer.

With this is connected a matter of more general import. There are those who say that insistence on the right techniques of singing and on the need for practice (even minimal) that goes with them takes away the spontaneous devotion of the people. There is too much artifice here, they say, the people, and perhaps even the choir, should be left to their own devices, they should be allowed to sing what they like (the 'old' favourites?) as they like. But spontaneity in *any* public performance is the recipe for chaos and ultimate disaster. The most skilled orchestra or choir (even the greatest) need to practise together under the leadership of an expert who has made the music his own and is able to convey his understanding of it to those who are to perform it. Yet they produce music that seems gloriously fresh, music that speaks to an audience but does so only because all the work of preparation and practice has gone before. Although we cannot look for a professional standard in parish choirs, we may not ask less of singers in church than is asked of those who perform secular concerts. Moreover, liturgy is a form of art and since it is concerned with the worship of God only the best may be offered to him. Every liturgical action, whether quiet and simple or large and elaborate, is a 'production' in the artistic sense, and if it is allowed to become a service that is slack, that lurches from one point to the next, the participants, whether people or choir or clergy, are inhibited from *praying*. On the other hand, a celebration that is well prepared, where all has been thought of beforehand, where the texts are clothed in appropriate music, enables everyone to pray and helps them to channel their prayer, their emotions and sentiments precisely because the pattern is clear and all is said and sung as well as possible. Above I have spoken of the need for recollection in public worship. Few things secure the possibility of recollection as a well prepared and well ordered service.

The Priest-Celebrant and Other Ministers

As with the choir, so with these. They have a service to render to the worshipping community. They are there to lead the people into prayer. The priest, it is true, has certain actions to perform that he alone can do, but as the president of the whole assembly he has a peculiarly important role to make it possible for the people to pray. And it needs to be said that his general bearing, his prayerfulness (though it is not a matter of wearing his devotion on his sleeve), his recollection, will be transmitted to the people. But both ministers and priest have certain texts to deliver and it is to these that we must now turn.

It is permissible for a layman to sing the phrases of the penitential rite (third form), to act as cantor or *psalmista* for the responsorial psalm and the Prayers of the Faithful and on Easter Eve to sing the *Exultet*. The priest-celebrant has certain texts to say or sing, notably the eucharistic prayer. How are these ministers to pray?

The principles that apply to the choir apply here too. They are ministers whose task it is to lead the community to prayer and they have to deliver texts that belong to them alone. Whether they are speaking or singing they have to attend to the rules that are required in either case. If a minister is rendering a sung text he must attend to the techniques that by its nature it demands. He must observe the 'rules'. Like the choir, he must prepare not only the musical text but the verbal one and if he does he will transmit to the people a chant that is the fruit of meditation and expertise. For prayer both are necessary; they cannot exist apart.

When we come to the priest-celebrant, since his role is all important, what has been said above applies with peculiar force to him. He is the indespensable minister, he more than anyone else is the servant of the community and he more than any others can lead the community into prayer and self-offering. Perhaps what needs to be realised more keenly is that he is exercising his pastoral office, in the very celebration of the liturgy he is serving the people. To do this he has certain texts to say and others to sing. The question is, how does he pray either kind? We need to recall Gelineau's distinction between merely saying a text and praying it. 'Saying' can be merely a coldly objective manner which suggests that the text is just so many words in a book that have to be read because they are in the book. Praying the text suggests that a celebrant has paid attention to the words previously and has made them his own; they come from him as words addressed to God that are calculated to lead the people to God. But if this effect is to be achieved the celebrant has to attend to the phrasing of the text in question, to line lengths, to punctuation marks and all that is required whenever one is speaking in public. Observance of the rules and attention to what he is saying is at the moment the celebrant's way of praying. The prayerful delivery of a text can make the people conscious of the presence of God and lead to prayer.

The case is not essentially different when he is singing a text. He has to attend to the chant, concentrate on the musical phrasing and on whatever other matters are necessary for an effective rendering of it. He is praying through what he is *doing*, and his prayer engages the whole of his personality since he is expressing the meaning of the prayer by mind and heart and voice. To this one may add that when he is praying in this fashion he will be reinforcing the message of the texts, he will be the means by which their meaning enters more deeply into the people's hearts; in a word, he will be leading them into prayer. But to do this as it should be done, he must learn the rules of singing, he must have mastered the musical text and must be able to sing it naturally and without strain. If he has no musical gifts, if his voice does not lend itself to singing, it would be better if he confined himself to a prayerful spoken delivery of the texts.

To sum up, for everyone, whether people, choir, ministers or priest, singing requires attention to the words sung, to the rules of music, the phrasing, the speed, the dynamics, the differing length of notes and so on. Attention to right singing is thus part of the prayer. Naturally, the more skilled the singer, the freer he will be to convey the meaning of what he has to sing. Like a good cricketer, he has no need to think all the time about the rules: he will sing quasi-instinctively. Not only, at best, do the words then become con-corporate with the music but the words-and-music become part of the singers whether they are congregation, choir or ministers. When I sing an Alleluia I do not think to myself that this word in Hebrew is *Hallel Yah* and means 'praise be to God'. I think of it as a joyful sound *through* which I give my praise to God. The same is true of other texts with more words and necessarily more notes (to put the matter at a rather low level) but once the habit of singing is acquired, the very song becomes a mode of prayer.

Song and prayer then can march together, and the better the singing, the more likely are the words to become prayer. To this we may add that the more apt the music for the words that are to be sung, and the more effectively the composer expresses the words according to their literary form and liturgical function, the better will be the prayer that comes from the combination of both. But this result demands not so much artifice as art and if the liturgy *can* do without art, most of us need it. Pius X is reported to have said that we must pray on beauty (*il faut prier sur la beauté*). Apt sounds, good sounds, beautiful sounds used in our worship can bring us closer to God who is the source of all beauty. Another saying, this time from Romano Guardini, takes the matter further. As long ago as 1930 in his little book *The Spirit of the Liturgy* he said that 'liturgy is life that has become art'. If one may gloss the text, this is to say that liturgy expresses life, the Christian life of the people of God, or even more broadly, it expresses the religious sense of human beings which however remains diffuse and vague until it is formed, given point and more definite meaning in what must be called a work of art. Art, as we all know, has its rules and exigencies. If we respect them, if to the best of our ability we find apt forms, we shall be providing channels into which the people can pour their worship and their prayer. Or rather, we shall be helping people in their often unconscious search for Truth, Goodness and Beauty which

> 'find their ultimate coherence and their most authentic glory in an Art that is sublime only because man is at work under the guidance of God. The most sublime action is at once the humblest of all: God hides himself and manifests himself under the

veil of signs and the faithful enter without violence or pride into the Tent of Meeting'.[1]

Among the most important of these signs is singing, but the signs cannot manifest the hidden God if they are unworthy of their purpose. They cannot 'speak' unless they are formed according to the rules that all art demands. But if they are, they can lead people to God.

1. *Communautés et Liturgies,* 1079, No.1, p.7.